Pelican Books
Knuckle Sandwich

David Robins was born in London in 1944. He has
been a teacher and lecturer, and a regular scriptwriter
for B.B.C. Schools. He worked with Philip Cohen on
the *Street Aid* research project into working-class youth
cultures, funded by the Leverhulme Trust. His reviews
and articles have appeared regularly in *Plays and Players*,
The Times, *Time Out*, *Radio Times* and other magazines,
and in addition he edited *Circuit* Magazine in 1968 and
Ink Newspaper in 1972. David Robins is currently gathering material for a book about young soccer fans, entitled *We Hate Humans*.

Philip Cohen was born in 1944 and educated at Queens'
College Cambridge. He set up *Street Aid* in 1970 and
since then has been a youth worker and community
organizer. His early research was on subculture theory,
and he worked with David Robins on the *Street Aid* research
project into working-class youth cultures, funded by the
Leverhulme Trust and concerned with the historical
analysis of working-class youth. His other publications on
the youth question include *Stopping the Wheels* (on
young workers and the labour movement); a handbook
for school leavers is currently in preparation.

David Robins and Philip Cohen

Knuckle Sandwich

Growing up in the
working-class city

Penguin Books

Penguin Books Ltd,
Harmondsworth, Middlesex, England
Penguin Books, 625 Madison Avenue,
New York, New York 10022, U.S.A.
Penguin Books Australia Ltd,
Ringwood, Victoria, Australia
Penguin Books Canada Ltd,
2801 John Street, Markham, Ontario, Canada L3R 1B4
Penguin Books (N.Z.) Ltd,
182–190 Wairau Road, Auckland 10, New Zealand

First published 1978

Made and printed in Great Britain by
Richard Clay (The Chaucer Press) Ltd,
Bungay, Suffolk
Set in Monotype Times

Contents

There is a street plan of the area of the Monmouth
estate on pages 14–15.

Acknowledgements

Most of the material for this book was gathered in the period from 1972 to 1974, while we were working on the Black Horse disco project. We kept notebooks and diaries, and made many hours of tape recordings with the young people we met. The core of the Youth Group referred to in Part One below consisted of ourselves, Martin Walker and Stuart Wooler. Much of the credit for the section dealing with the travails of local tenants associations – 'Divided We Stand' – must go to Stuart Wooler, who helped put it together.

In the two years following the Black Horse episode, we conducted a full-scale research project into working-class youth cultures, under the auspices of Street Aid, the Covent Garden youth agency. The research project was funded by the Leverhulme Trust. Our thanks to the staff and trustees of Street Aid for supporting our work, and to the late Lord Holford of the Leverhulme Trust for his receptiveness and enthusiasm.

Lucy Bland helped to research much of the data relating to the age and location of young soccer fans. David Zane Mairowitz adapted the Brecht poem 'Praise of Learning'. Dick Pountain drew the map and diagrams. Leslie Corner and Hazel Nash typed most of the manuscript. Special thanks to all of them, and to Hilary Woodward and Chris Allen, exemplary comrades.

Last, but certainly not least, Dr David Downes, Senior Lecturer in Social Administration at the London School of Economics, supervised our work and gave much-needed advice and criticism. We owe a special debt of gratitude to him.

D.R.
P.C.

Introduction

This book begins with an account of an attempt to establish a youth centre on a large working-class estate in North London, which took place between September 1972 and April 1974. The centre was named after the converted pub which housed it – the Black Horse.

We hope there may be lessons to be learnt here for people involved in similar work, in contexts similar to the one we describe.

Part Two of this book consists of a series of short portraits of life in this tough inner city area; each focuses on the chains of cultural transmission through which this neighbourhood's internal divisions are reproduced, and the way this is registered in and on the configurations of its youth underlife.

In Part Three we return to the scene of the Black Horse disco two years after its closure. Many tenants are demanding the closure of a black youth centre, while in the local elections white youths flock to vote for the National Front. In the light of such developments, we advance the case for breaking with the whole problematic of 'youth leisure provision' and for abandoning the traditional models of socialist youth organization. We go on to set out the terms of a new strategy of social education based on the affinity groups of working-class youth, and aimed at releasing their capacities as teachers and spokesmen of their peers. We point to the creation of possible new sources of youth leadership, for example, young tenants associations – and new sources of mediation between children's and parents' culture. The post-script, 'Figures in a Political Landscape', illustrates the decline of working-class socialism and the growth of right-wing populism among the young.

5

Introduction

Throughout we have changed the names of the people who feature in our stories. In most cases we have altered the names of streets, pubs, clubs and so on as well. We did this to protect the people involved, and their neighbourhood.

David Robins
Philip Cohen
July 1977

Prologue

Educationalists base their conclusions about the state of the nation's youth on what happens in the classroom during school hours; employers make their deductions from what they see on the shop floor during working hours; psychologists talk about adolescence and the crisis of identity, concentrating on who did what to whom during those first five years in the family; police spokesmen, social workers, and public moralists worry about what youth get up to in the evenings, weekends, and other less official holidays from family, school, and work. Each has their own particular axe to grind, even if none are in a position to see the whole picture. But how do young people themselves experience growing up in the working-class city?

Ask the pre-1950s generation, and the majority answer comes back loud and clear. Growing up is essentially an apprenticeship to work. Accounts of family life are filled with material details of working life, your parents', the jobs you did, both in the home and outside, while still at school, your own first experiences as a wage-earner. Even recreation may be purposefully related to the disciplines of work for the aspiring, while holidays are pressed into the service of supplementing the family incomes of those less well off.

With the post-war generations, though, the answers are much more equivocal. For a minority, especially those living in the older industrial areas, the traditional apprenticeships may still hold, along with the economic institution itself. For the rest, and especially those living in the inner city, the accounts of childhood and youth are increasingly dominated by the themes of free time, rather than labour time. For some, every sector of experience may come to be measured against how much or little purchase it affords on that kind of autonomy.

Prologue

Yet such accounts are also forced to recognize that the key to the freedom of the working-class city is not a birthright, not for free, because the key is still the wage. And to earn a wage means to be subject to all the traditional unfreedoms of labouring under Capital. Just as the laws of a market economy demand the free circulation of commodities (including the commodity that is labour power), so everything that takes place in free time remains a consolation prize for the unfreedoms of the labour process.

From the vantage-point of many working-class youth, as long as you aren't washing floors in a detention centre, as long as you have still got a few bob in your pocket, and can go out and have a good time with your friends, then you are still free. You're free to walk the long way through the park instead of wasting precious pence on a bus, to save your money and get some enjoyment at the same time. You're free to smoke yourself to death, or get drunk. And you have the greatest freedom of all, to fall in love with a girl or boy of your choice, to get married and have children. As long as you can do all this, you can go on believing you live in a free society, where after all the best things in life are free. And you will defend those freedoms to the last, against both those who would try and curtail them, and those who would tell you that they are illusory, and only serve to conceal the real unfreedoms from you.

What the youth wage does buy, at least, is freedom from school, from the parental nags – 'it costs so much to feed him these days I'll be glad when he starts work'. You can at last afford to buy your own cigarettes and beer, no more cadging from older brothers and sisters. You're a young worker, not a school *kid* living on pocket-money and paper rounds. No wonder so many can't wait to get out of an institution which is increasingly experienced as a fruitless imposition, a waste of good labour time, something clapped on to your life from above.

What the youth wage does *not* buy, though, is independence from home. It's only because they go on living with their parents, their subsistence needs subsidized out of the family wage, that young workers can earn less, but still have more to spend on enjoying themselves, than their elders. Yet this can create its own problems, its own pressures to early marriage. Those who try and set up on their own, without an adult, i.e. family wage, will quickly discover the difference between the full cost of their maintenance, and the board and lodge they have been paying to mum. Relative affluence shrivels up the moment they walk out of the parental door.

The assertion of youthful independence conforms to the fundamental class divide. On one side, those who embrace studenthood, accept continued wageless dependence, on their families or State grants, and whose struggle is for *a place of their own to be who they like in*. On the other, those who take for granted the fact of continued domestic dependence, because their target is *a wage of their own to do what they like with*. If dependence and autonomy are conditional on one another, so is the tension between the two. Working-class youth also demand places of their own – to do what they like with – but these places are not flats, but discos, or youth clubs, or the football terraces. They use their wage to buy substitutes for the thing they lack.

Is it necessary for *youth* to come up against the whole apparatus of the State in order to lay claim to these freedoms? Does this apparatus merely guarantee their rights and obligations as *citizens*, or does it also confirm them in their unfreedom as *workers*? Is the State educational system just the school, or does it also include the police, the welfare and penal systems? However much they may disconnect their confrontations with Capital and the State, however much they may push these experiences into the background of a consciousness focused elsewhere, aren't these the forces which determine their lives, including that response?

Those who continue to move within the bounds of an occupational culture, can more easily make the connections between the different sectors of growing up; here is how one young Irish building worker described his transition from school to work:

The situation on the factory floor isn't so very different as in school. You have to work in school, you call the teachers Sir, the bell goes when you've got to start, the bell goes when you have your teabreak, the bell goes when you have your dinner. You're told what to wear . . . Schoolkids in school, if they rebel against the school system, are immediately picked out as individuals, they're taken in front of the headmaster, and either caned, given a good telling off, or expelled. Now this isn't very different from what goes on, on the shop floor. If you aren't satisfied with your conditions and you want more money, if you go into the office, the boss would just turn round and laugh; if you're late you get a bollocking, and so on . . .

This lad knew what to expect on the shop floor long before he ever got there from his dad, his dad's workmates, his older brothers and their friends. He could judge his school experience against that measure because he was connected to the informal labour exchange, which circulates information not just about the jobs going, but wages and conditions, what are the good and bad firms to work for, as part of the local grapevines of the working-class city. Those who are most adept at classroom guerrilla warfare, may also find the transition to work easiest. Their 'bad' school record ensures that they are forced into the kind of unskilled work where 'mucking about', leaning on brooms, and other means of resisting the impositions of boredom and routine, are an integral and accepted part of shop-floor culture. These jobs may have been decasualized, but the attitude of young workers to them has not.

But not everyone is so 'fortunate'. The break-up of occupational communities, the changing structure of the inner-city labour market, means that many have no family precedents, or wider source of knowledge and support to draw on. As one girl put it:

The one thing I found, they throw you out, you haven't got a clue what to expect, they just throw you out as raw material. There's no preparation in school, you just have to find your feet, because in your working life, you're really on your own. If you've got no one to turn to in your place of work, it can be a pretty frightening experience.

Most young workers' experience lie between these two extremes. But as the inner-city economy becomes dominated by white-collar jobs, where the emphasis is on the cultivation of middle-class manners, not proletarian solidarities, the transition to work may become an area of real discontinuity, and for those least able to compete, of structural unemployment, and enforced free time.

Exposure to some labour processes may be enough in themselves to jar against the expectations formed elsewhere, though here the unfreedoms perceived in labour time may only reinforce all the more strongly the hope of a liberation whose promise can never be fulfilled.

The following account is by a young print worker. It is neither more nor less typical of contemporary work experiences in the inner city, but perhaps it may serve better than most to illustrate the terms of the problem, and the background to this book:

I left school when I was fifteen, and I got myself a job in the print shop. And it was really good, you know, the first day in the working world. The boss I had was a really nice guy, and he promised me, because I didn't have an apprenticeship, I was like a trainee, that I'd be O.K. and that I'd get on and things would be really dandy. And I believed him, because he had a nice smile and that. And I was quite happy at this job for a number of years. I was paid a pittance really. But I was told that every birthday you would get a rise, and every six months and all that . . . but the rises were very small and sometimes they didn't come at all. I thought maybe it was because I wasn't being a good boy . . . but I was really doing the work, you know. As I got a bit older and learnt a bit more about printing, the boss didn't seem to want to appreciate the experience I had gained. He kept on leading me on with the same old story that 'well you're not quite old enough yet' . . . and I believed him and thought to myself, 'Well, I'll carry on', because I knew that I was developing a skill and I knew that this was my career and I've got to make the best of it. A new machine would come in. Another young guy would start. And that's how it went on for a few years. And then I looked around the shop one day and there was nothing but school kids there. And they were all doing work that guys old enough to get a good wage were doing. And they were being told the same lies. And I started to open my eyes up a bit. And the crunch came one day when this new guy came in and we were all talking about wages (we didn't have a teabreak) while we were washing our hands at the end of the day. And he was earning about three pounds more than all the other guys, some of whom were about two years older, and they didn't like it. And of course I didn't like it either, so we got together and marched into the office and complained about it. They tried to cool

Prologue

us down by saying the guy was being paid travelling expenses and things like that. I started to get angry in myself. Just as I was going to make the grade to become qualified – if you can call it that because I wouldn't have had any papers to say so – so the crunch came one day and I got the sack. I really started worrying about it, you know, what am I going to do now? But as soon as I got out of the door, after all the bother over the last couple of years, it was like a big weight off my back. I really felt free when I walked out of those doors . . .

Part One
The Fall of
the Black Horse Disco

When new housing estates began to go up
after the war . . . family after family moved
out of the old Edwardian or Victorian rows
into the new little boxes. It was all right . . .
But when they looked around for the pub there
wasn't one! And no fish and chip saloon!
That was the catch in it.

Jack Common.
The Freedom of the Streets

Monmouth and Denby estates (1972-4)

SHOPS

MAIN ROAD

CAFE

SHOPS

'248' DISCO

SHOPS SHOPS SHOPS SHOPS

To
RIVERSIDE
SPORTS
CENTRE

CAMBRIA
HOUSE

MERIONETH DRIVE

MONMOUTH
ESTATE (GLC)

SNOWDON HOUSE

CAERPHILLY
WAY

THE
BLACK
HORSE

NEW FLATS STARTIN

BLACK HORSE STREET

UHURU BLACK
YOUTH CENTRE

SECONDARY SCHOOL

ADVENTURE
PLAYGROUND

DISUSED RAILWAY LAND

DEMOLITION
SITE

STEELYARD FREE SCHOOL

DEMOLITION SITE

MEREDITH NEIGHBOURHOOD
ADVICE CENTRE

MAIN ROAD

KEY: ▓▓▓ Principal foci of activity in text   ▨▨▨ Places referred to in text

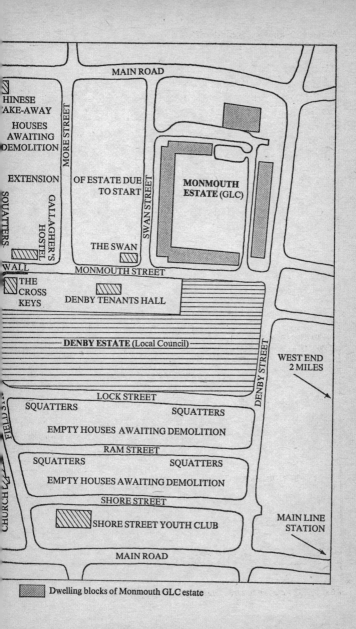

CHINESE TAKE-AWAY

HOUSES AWAITING DEMOLITION

EXTENSION OF ESTATE DUE TO START

MAIN ROAD

MORE STREET

SWAN STREET

MONMOUTH ESTATE (GLC)

SQUATTERS

GALLAGHER'S HOSTEL

THE SWAN

WALL

MONMOUTH STREET

THE CROSS KEYS

DENBY TENANTS HALL

DENBY ESTATE (Local Council)

DENBY STREET

WEST END 2 MILES

LOCK STREET

SQUATTERS   SQUATTERS

FIELD ST

EMPTY HOUSES AWAITING DEMOLITION

RAM STREET

SQUATTERS   SQUATTERS

CHURCH

EMPTY HOUSES AWAITING DEMOLITION

SHORE STREET

SHORE STREET YOUTH CLUB

MAIN LINE STATION

MAIN ROAD

Dwelling blocks of Monmouth GLC estate

Friends and Neighbours

Monmouth estate is a 'new' GLC estate: it was first occupied in 1960 and is still (1977) uncompleted. It is a low-density estate with a mixture of low- and high-rise blocks whose names evoke the wild expanses of the Welsh mountains: Snowdonia, Cambria, Merioneth. The area on which the estate was built lies sandwiched between two main arterial highways in North London. In the era of the railway boom of the nineteenth century it was colonized by Irish labouring families and, being close to the main railway it has remained a classic reception area for immigrants – Scots, Greeks, West Indians, Cypriots. A transitory population. Run-down lodging-houses, beer halls, gambling, and prostitution, a red-light district of its own. To this day officially designated as a twilight zone, with high rates of delinquency, mental breakdown and suicide, the area has nevertheless enjoyed strong traditions of trade-unionism, particular among its railway and building workers, and more recently was one of the strongholds of the movement against the Rent Act of 1957, and the St Pancras rent strikes of 1959–61. When some local rent strikers were evicted, unofficial twenty-four-hour stoppages took place in near-by railway goods depots and building sites.

The area therefore contained the elements of a strong occupational community, but since the war large-scale redevelopments have led to the mass deportation of families, and the links between the associations of the workplace and neighbourhood have irrevocably broken down. On the new estate most families have been brought in from all over London, while others have been rehoused from another part of the borough. A lot of the conflicts which feature so prominently in this story have to be

17

The Fall of the Black Horse Disco

understood historically in terms of this uneasy mix of the 'established' and 'outsiders'.

This planned residential ghetto, surrounded on all sides by thundering lorries and desolated goods yards, was only a short bus ride away from the West End, but the pervading sense of isolation seemed to immobilize all sections of the community. Twelve hundred families lived there, in large two-floor maisonettes which were generally very comfortable and well-cared-for. Indeed the estate reflects the familiar contrast between the private trappings of affluence – colour TVs, kitchen units, and fitted carpets – and public squalor – halls and stairways strewn with garbage, and covered with graffiti, lifts that don't work and telephone boxes smashed up. Apart from the few remaining pubs, squatting uneasily where old street corners used to be, there was nowhere for groups of neighbours to meet together even if they wanted to.

In the middle of the estate, as if stranded by the tide of 'progress', stood the old public-house, the Black Horse. A solid-looking building, with a large ground floor for business, a huge cellar, and two upper floors which had served as living quarters. The pub was scheduled for demolition, like so much else in the neighbourhood, and there were vague GLC promises of a community centre being built there in a few years' time. Then one of the young volunteers working on the Adventure Playground site adjoining the pub started to put round the idea that the Black Horse should be saved from destruction. He put up a notice in its windows: 'The GLC promises us a Community Centre in 1976. Why wait that long? Let's use the Black Horse NOW.'

Although the Monmouth estate no longer had an official tenants association, there was the Open Space Committee, formed a few years earlier when a group of tenants had banded together to force the local Council to provide a play site. The Committee saw the possibilities in saving the pub, but in order for it to be saved it would have to be occupied immediately, judging by the speed with which other empty buildings had been stripped, wrecked, or gutted. Through somewhat devious channels some squatters living near by, many of whom were facing eviction, were

18

approached. At the beginning of March 1973, the squatters met the Open Space Committee, and it was agreed that the occupation would have their backing. The Committee wanted a community hall and a stick to beat the council with, the squatters wanted a place to live. It was agreed that the squatters could have the top floor as their own private quarters; they would also act as caretakers for the building as a whole.

The squatters group then went from door to door round the estate to explain what was happening. Most tenants followed the line of the squatters' arguments but seemed fairly indifferent. Others grew indignant at the mere mention of the Council and the lack of amenities in the area, and took the doorstep visit as a chance to have a good old beef about the disgraceful state of things generally. A regular party started up on one floor and soon the whole corridor was filled with laughing, joking women. The visit was a welcome relief from housebound monotony, and the Black Horse was forgotten in the general hilarity. Although the Black Horse action confused some people, who found it hard to 'place' after a hard day's work, the door-to-door campaign encouraged the squatters. Many people seemed impressed by the fact that they had come and in effect *asked their permission* first. There were very few openly hostile to the idea.

The night after the door-to-door visits, the Black Horse was squatted, quietly and efficiently, with no interference from the police and with full acceptance by the local children, who had been forewarned. John Stephens, a young man who lived with his parents on the Monmouth, had brought round a van which he used in his new job. The presence of this local support helped to win the confidence of the children, who started to gather round the Black Horse when the van appeared; and they even organized a lookout to warn the squatters if the police should appear in the vicinity.

The police may have decided to keep a 'low profile'. A few days later the local bobby, Constable Groves, who worked in a youth centre in Shore Street in the evenings, came round on a 'friendly' visit. After giving the squatters the benefit of his cynicism – 'It'll never happen, the kids round here behave like

19

anmals' – he left satisfied that it was nothing to do with the police, unless they were asked to intervene.

This was the first time in this neighbourhood that a squat had been undertaken with the full knowledge of the tenants and the active backing of some sections. Squatting had been employed as a tactic by the people on this estate to get what they wanted, and the interests of squatters and local people were, in theory at least, complementary.

Of course, the Open Space Committee's position was more contradictory than that. The day after the occupation the Committee took what was for them a big step in the dark. They held the first of their regular weekly meetings in the ground floor of the old pub. 'Are we breaking the law?' A justification had to be found: 'we're here in lieu of negotiations with the GLC.' The squatting question, the principle of squatting as the right way to get what you want, was embarrassedly by-passed. The Committee called the squatters caretakers, never referring to them as squatters.

Despite this caution, the Committee were determined to hold on to what they had gained. The action was justifiable and irrevocable. There would be no backing down. The Committee wrote an open letter, clearly stating their support for the squatters *as caretakers* of the Black Horse. This was handed over as a guarantee of their support if the GLC came round asking questions. Were the squatters being used as pawns? One thing is clear: the belligerence with which even the most conservative of working-class community organizations will hold on to what they have gained through struggle, however little. A sectional as opposed to class interest.

Although the Black Horse was squatted little more than two weeks after the landlord moved out, this wasn't the first time it had been reoccupied. The children had got in there first. Indeed it was only with their approval that the squatting group moved in at all. Permission had been secured through the playground workers, who had had a meeting with the children. It was pointed out that, if the squatters didn't go in, 'it'll be knocked down and then no one will be able to use it'. However, the children agreed to the occupation only because it was stressed that when the pub had been renovated they would get it back, or, more exactly, it would be properly run partly for their benefit. The squatters were only there to make sure that this would happen. The children were adamant that the Black Horse should not be a place where 'hippies all live together'. As far as they were concerned, it could never be a private house. And sure enough it wasn't. As the squatters settled in, they had to point out to the kids constantly that they, as caretakers, should have privacy. However, the children suspected that any attempt to insist on the minimum privacy necessary to lead a decent life was really a way of keeping them out and reneging on the deal. So living in the Black Horse was something of a nightmare, a constant battle to keep the kids out. It was like living in the playground of a turbulent primary school.

The presence of the playground workers also ensured that the squatters were bracketed in the same category as them in the children's eyes, and not only the children's. Young and old tended to see the 'community worker' as understanding, well spoken, soft – either an ineffectual mug who 'lets kids crawl all over him day and night' or, in the case of a person with sufficient personal charisma, a saint who can do no wrong and whose name is remembered after he leaves. There had been one such legendary figure already, and the squatters were constantly asked whether they were his friends. To say yes was a passport to acceptance. The squatters tried to make it clear they were neither saints nor mugginses. They resolved that the first priority was to make the place secure against invaders, whoever they might be. Nevertheless the children managed to worm their way by hook or by permission into the building.

From their earliest years the children* could remember only

---

* The groups of children were always put in charge of the older girls in their substitute-mum capacity. The boys, however, tended to break away from these mixed groups and form their own junior street gangs. This release of boys from child-minding obligations, and the reinforcement of this role for girls, is the basic way in which the division of labour on a sexual basis

houses being knocked down, streets and familiar landmarks disappearing under a haze of smoke and brickdust, to be replaced by narrow mazes of corrugated-iron fencing. The Black Horse had been a place to stash your stolen property, start fires, run amok, do exactly what you wanted to do. Compared to the Black Horse, the Adventure Playground appeared as what it was, a sop. Play on the Adventure, keep out from under our feet. Few children used the Adventure Playground regularly. Why did they need a simulated bomb site, when they had so many real ones all around?

The generally acclaimed leader of the 8-to-13s was a charming manic and unpredictable thirteen-year-old, Billy Sheahan. Billy's family lived in one of the last of the slums that were still sprinkled here and there around the estate awaiting clearance. A legendary 'job' had made Billy his reputation. He broke into a local youth club and did £2,000 of damage, but first he broke into an iron-monger's to get the tools to do the damage with! Following this Billy was placed in the care of the local authority. He was on the run from approved school when he led the children's occupation of the old pub. He reserved one room as his 'den'. Another room was used specifically for shitting and pissing and also as a hallmark of Billy's tenancy. As Lord of this particular manor, Billy didn't take too kindly to the invasion of his territory by hippies or 'no, all right, you're not hippies, but I'm not quite sure what you are!' Consider the following scenario: as darkness falls, Billy and his mates slip into the shadows out of sight of the cruising police patrol cars. Pockets filled with the booty of the day, they look for an old deri to spend the night in together. Every tube station in North London and some even further afield (Billy was smart enough to travel to work) had his name scrawled on its walls. BILLY SHEAHAN WAS HERE. BILLY RULES. Or simply B. SHEAHAN.

---

is instituted for the next generation. One consequence of this is that boys become the main bearers of street tradition – their presence is continuous from childhood to adolescence – whereas the girls are forced to the periphery.

It's easy to see why some people romanticize these types. Revolutionary outlaw or self-defeating criminal? In our eyes Billy was in training as an apprentice gangster, a known criminal, the bloke you went to school with and whose name henceforth will act as a kind of reference point in defining the relative hardness of your area. One of the squatters asked Billy what it was like at approved school. 'It's all right, they're strict, but they've got to be, haven't they? Until they put me in a *stronger* place . . .'

In contrast to the children, the older youth showed little interest n the Black Horse and its embattled occupants, apart from the odd carelessly lobbed brick. They showed even less interest in the growing controversy surrounding it. To them, the Black Horse was ' just a dump. What do you want to live in there for? Ain't you got homes to go to?' As for the Open Space Committee, there was the suspicion that they were 'a bunch of thieves, on the make, they're just in it for themselves'.

Such attitudes expressed both the typical teenage disassociation from parental concerns and a prejudice common among their parents. Why would any section of local people want to form themselves into a committee, put themselves on the firing line if things go wrong, do all that unpaid work, if it wasn't for a desire to 'rule' their neighbours or appropriate the finances? Certainly if a tenants association or committee does not have a strong base, it quickly becomes identified as a clique and suspicions grow. The actual status of the Open Space Committee, however, seemed beyond repute. Long-established local families in the main, they were undoubtedly the 'top firm', at least in their part of the estate. As long-serving locals, they felt justified in asserting their superiority. As one of them put it: 'Unless you've been born and brought up round here, you have no right to speak about how the area should be run.' The Committee also had their own moral credentials to go along with these ethnic ones. They did not drink, for example, and refused to enter the pub across the road to the Black Horse, the Cross Keys, or even consider doing committee business over a few pints.

The Cross Keys was the recognized headquarters of the local villains, the fraternity of scrap men, fences, shotgun merchants –

another reason why the Committee would not go into it. (It offended their code of moral respectability – not one that was forged out of any deference to middle-class decency, however; it was more that they had a position to keep up.) The fact that the Cross Keys was often the quietest pub in the neighbourhood, and that the brewers had withdrawn their franchise on the place, made some tenants suspect that the landlord must be involved in some close working relationship with his customers. Ironically, the local villains had an interest in the Black Horse that made the children's interest seem half-hearted by comparison. It was well known they were after the lead and timber contained in the old building. This was one of the main reasons why the Committee had backed the squat, to prevent the roof mysteriously disappearing one night.

There was another section of the 'dangerous classes' where 'trouble' was to be expected from: this was the 'Gallagher lads', who frequented the public bar of the Cross Keys. Old man Gallagher ran a lodging-house across the road to the Cross Keys for Southern Irish boys who came to work in the building trade and for old dossers. By all accounts, Gallagher ran a tight racket and exploited his clients for whatever he could get out of them. He had made a considerable fortune in this rough trade. The area surrounding the Black Horse was considered dangerous largely because of these lads' presence. Before it closed the Black Horse had been their main drinking place. Unlike the Cross Keys it had been rough inside. A few weeks before closure, the public bar had been the scene of a stand-up fight between the Irish lads and some black workers living in the vicinity. The reputation of the Black Horse as a dangerous and undesirable place to go remained with it to some degree after it closed for business and opened for the community.

The squatters' nerves were soon tested to the full by the vivid bouts of street violence that took place regularly on Friday and Saturday nights. One Saturday evening, for example, a thirty-strong gang of lads – not teenagers, but young men in their twenties and thirties – launched a noisy attack on Gallagher's hostel. (Gang violence of this kind should in no way be confused with the violence of the younger people.) Bricks were thrown, windows smashed, police panda cars patrolled for the rest of the night. A taste of Northern Ireland . . .

Gallagher's hostel was due for demolition. Before this happened, a deputation of the Irish lads called round to see the squatters. We were understandably nervous about this unscheduled visit, but apart from reminiscing about the fights they'd had in the bar, they exuded nothing more frightening than Southern Irish affability. Apparently, old man Gallagher encouraged his boys to take a hand in constructive community work. It turned out that some of the visiting party had helped level the site of the Adventure Playground. Now they had come to offer their services to the Black Horse, and they were as good as their word. They saw their involvement in the place as a way of giving themselves some stake in the area, which they had never had before. Squatters and Gallaghers were natural allies since both faced similar problems of gaining acceptance. But the presence of Gallagher's lads in the Black Horse angered the Open Space Committee and horrified a lot of other people.

It was clear from all this that marginal groups which became too actively involved around the Black Horse alienated others, and the pub and its occupants had become the focus of several competing interest groups, not to mention the Council.

The GLC Councillor, Grimes, made a surprise visit early on in the occupation. Grimes, who ran the timber yard on the corner, was worried about his falling reputation in the area. As one tenant put it: 'The bloody Labour Party didn't even bother to put a leaflet through our door for the local elections, they're so complacent about our support. We vote for them almost a hundred per cent round here and what do they do in return? Nothing.' Grimes was impressed by the show of tenant militancy around the Black Horse and the anger it provoked about the lack of social amenities. A community centre in two years' time was hardly a vote-catching slogan.

Grimes met the Open Space Committee and promised that the GLC would review its plans to demolish the old pub, provided the squatters were removed forthwith. 'They've got no legal right to be there.' The Committee refused; beside they weren't squatters, they were caretakers. 'But do they all live up there together? The men and the women.' The Committee refused to be sidetracked. They may have shared the Councillor's prejudices, but they weren't going to hand over control of the building. Grimes's final statement was 'All right, you can have the building, and we won't take action to evict the squatters, but you have to agree to be out by the end of the year so we can review our plans freely.' The Committee saw Grimes's climb-down as a partial victory.

For several of the squatter-caretakers, the occupation of the Black Horse had destroyed forever the fashionable mythologies of the working-class community. Libertarian Socialists with their vision of Power to that irreducible phenomenon the People are wrong in seeing the working-class community as some kind of homogeneous grouping, a unified ahistorical structure, rather than as a dynamic and complex organization developed in response to specific conditions. Some of us, however, clung to the belief in a homogeneous community: the Black Horse could become a centre which everyone would eventually muck in and run together without leaders and as equals in the struggle against capitalism. But as we have shown, in so far as there was a community on the Monmouth, it was hardly such a one-dimensional affair but the complex result of the inhabitants' many-sided attempts to organize themselves and of the planners' and bureaucrats' attempts to organize and control them.

Ironically, one of the main attractions of community work for non-aligned socialists has been that it is relatively unpoliced. The unions have got the struggle at the point of production under control, the political parties command the terrain of national class politics; the community is less well colonized, or rather it was until the intervention of the myriad community organizations. In this borough alone, there were over sixty statutory and voluntary social welfare agencies. A 'problem' neighbourhood like the Monmouth is simply crawling with 'soft-cops', from probation officers to detached youth workers, and agents of the Community

Development Commission. Professional community workers, however, armed with a sociological training, and often a long-term presence in the area, operate with a much more sophisticated model of the community than the 'revolutionaries'. Their professional ideology aims at supporting attempts at local self-organization, by integrating them with the local State apparatus *in order to make it work*. Community workers are committed, structurally, and whatever their personal politics, to a kind of Fabianism from below. The focus for this approach on the Monmouth was the Meredith Neighbourhood Centre, which was set up by a special committee of the Council. The Centre's task was to co-ordinate local pressure groups into neighbourhood forums and from this to develop a series of 'working parties' on issues such as housing, redevelopment, play space and amenities: a kind of neighbourhood council, with even fewer teeth. What was involved was the creation of an *intermediate bureaucracy*, between working-class organizations and local government. As such its political position was supposed to be strictly 'neutral', looking at 'both sides' of a problem, representing each to the other, and giving the unorganized access to information, advice and guidance as to their 'rights'.

But this strategy of mediation met with some unexpected resistance. As the Centre's report put it, in somewhat aggrieved tones: 'Many people have expressed to us a sort of "us" and "them" viewpoint of local government, regarding it as just another giant obstacle in the way of improving the quality of their lives, instead of the mechanism through which that improvement could be made.' Despite its sophistication – and its sophistries about 'participation' and 'involvement' community development remains essentially opportunistic.

Nothing could have been less opportunistic than the offer of Harry, an electrician, to rewire the Black Horse in his own time and at his own expense, and to supervise the groups of children let in from time to time to help in the clearing-up work.

Harry was a widower who lived alone. He had no kids of his own, but enjoyed their company as much as they did his. In the

27

evenings he worked in a youth club as an unpaid helper. But the the sight of a small, bespectacled, middle-aged man entering the Black Horse with parties of children set people talking. Why should a man who doesn't even live on the estate volunteer to do something for nothing? The general conclusion was that he must be perverted.The children were amused by these rumours, and some took great delight in playing up to their parents' fears. But there was absolutely no substance to the allegations.

Truth or lies, it didn't matter. The Open Space Committee put pressure on the caretakers, who had to tactfully ask him to leave. The tragedy is that in contrast to professional community workers, who do it for a living, the good intentions of people like Harry can only qualify them for a role in their community's theatre of deviance. Fortunately, Harry was got off the stage before the audience started pelting him with rotten apples.

The diagrams on the following pages attempt to map the degree of distance and relation between different groups as a function of their level of interest in the Black Horse.

These diagrams can be read as snapshots taken at different points in time showing the rough political geography of the area, and the dynamics of invasion–succession–dominance in relation to the pub.

For diagramatic purposes, we have used the crude distinction between 'roughs' and 'respectables'.

Confrontation

The spring of 1973 saw the Monmouth Open Space Committee firmly in the saddle of the Black Horse. Councillor Grimes, the advances of Little Billy Sheahan, Gallagher's boys *et al.* had been, if only temporarily, repulsed. The caretakers, who had borne the brunt of all this infighting, began in different ways to reappraise their role. Some stayed on to help with the building work. Others couldn't stand the constant invasion of their privacy and moved out of the building; but they decided to go on working on the

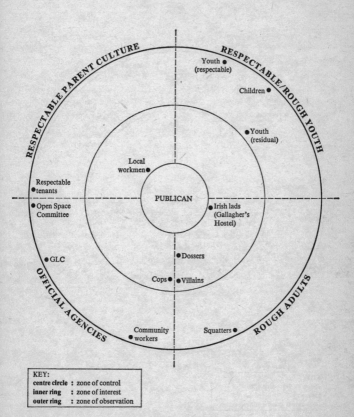

RESPECTABLE PARENT CULTURE

RESPECTABLE/ROUGH YOUTH

OFFICIAL AGENCIES

ROUGH ADULTS

Youth
(respectable) ●

Children ●

● Youth
(residual)

Local
workmen ●

PUBLICAN

● Irish lads
(Gallagher's
Hostel)

Respectable
● tenants

● Open Space
Committee

● GLC

● Dossers

Cops ● ● Villains

Community
● workers

Squatters ●

KEY:
centre circle : zone of control
inner ring : zone of interest
outer ring : zone of observation

Black Horse: Public house (September 1972).

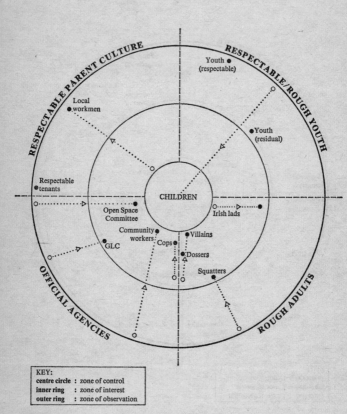

Black Horse: Empty (January 1973). Awaiting demolition.

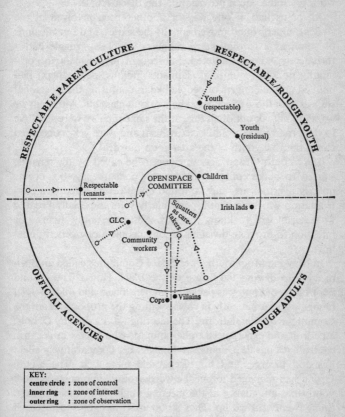

Black Horse: Squatted (March 1973).

project. What was the most useful contribution they could make? They were teachers and youth workers, and it seemed natural to work for some youth provision in the Black Horse.

All of us had in one way or another been involved in the student underground movements of the sixties, and our illusions of youth as a revolutionary vanguard of class struggle had – fortunately – been shattered. Subsequent involvement in community politics (squatting, claimants' unions, newspapers) had pointed up the dangers of people like us confusing their personal stances with those engendered by working-class life. Although we wanted to break out of all this, at the same time we were sensitive to the broad issue of adult chauvinism and were very concerned to see that the youth of the area got a fair deal.

The 'Youth Group', as we came to be called by the tenants, started to make contact with its new constituency, but events quickly overtook us, and we found ourselves involved in a confrontation which we didn't particularly want, especially because we'd hardly got to know the kids. And it certainly wasn't our intention to provoke divisions among people along generational lines.

In May the Monmouth Open Space Committee called an open meeting to discuss the future of the Black Horse. The ground floor of the old pub was packed with pensioners and middle-aged mums, who sat patiently in rows awaiting the proposals from the Committee on the platform. The meeting was chaired by Dennis, an adroit and experienced trade-unionist, who kept it under firm control. Alongside Dennis sat Maggie, her comparatively silent husband George, and his inseparable mate Len. The Youth Group had managed to put the word around among some older youth that attendance at the meeting might be in their interest. Some twenty turned up. They stood apart in twos and threes at the back of the hall, and watched with silent suspicion.

Dennis and Maggie proceeded to tell the tenants about the work they had been doing on their behalf. Plans for the structural conversion of the Black Horse had been made, money had been promised from the Council. The Youth Group had fears that the need for some provision for older youth would be overlooked.

After nearly an hour of mainly platform talk, it was clear that these fears were justified. We decided to intervene.

Some of us went to put the word around among the kids. What came out of the conversation was that, if together we got the Committee to agree, we could run a disco in the basement; not a make-shift youth club disco, with a few old chairs and tables and a coke machine, but something 'really smart, a bit of the West End in the Black Horse'. There was a lot of enthusiasm and a lot of wild talk about how to raise money to finance the venture. While the meeting dragged on, a group of the most enthusiastic kids went down with one of the Youth Group to survey the basement. The idea of being the first-in hard core that would run the place with us obviously appealed. There were offers to clear up the place and renovate it. One of the boys was a self-employed builder with his dad, and he put his services on the line. The girls had more particular ideas about how the place should be decorated. The walls should be painted exciting colours, there should be 'mood' lighting and so on. There would be no trouble in the disco because 'we'll defend it if any other mobs try and take it'.

While the dream of the disco was taking shape in the basement, the tenants were still being lectured to upstairs about problems with the Council, and the last thought in their minds was a disco. Not only that, most of the people at the meeting had come out of impatience, anger, or concern at conditions on the estate generally, and did not see the specific issue of the future of the Black Horse as particularly relevant to them.

The nascent disco lobby rejoined the meeting and interrupted the speeches to announce their plans. The audience listened bewildered. We stressed the need to get the kids involved in a place of their own so that they would not cause so much trouble on the estate. Some murmured that that was a good idea. Most complained about noise, vandalism and so on. The very idea of 'teenagers' seemed to provoke them.

John Stephens, who had helped squat the Black Horse at the beginning and had been encouraged to come to the meeting, got really angry at the reaction and started shouting insults. For him, a young man in his early twenties, born and brought up in the area and looked up to by the younger kids as something of a style-leader, this meeting represented the reality of his so-called community. 'The struggle of workers at home as well as at work? Don't make me laugh! A community association dominated by crabby old ladies with their hairdos, handbags and big mouths . . . You'll never be able to do anything with this place as long as that lot interfere. They'll hound you every time you make a move, the fucking old bags!'

After delivering this verdict, he stormed out of the hall in disgust. The other kids were also angered by the reception accorded to their disco, but they were much more defensive, wary of getting into a fight with the 'mums'.

The Youth Group pointed out that we were getting nowhere fast and suggested that a meeting for those interested in the disco should get under way immediately upstairs. This suggestion was well received – and by the tenants, who wanted to get on with business. The meeting that followed was predictably chaotic, everyone talking at cross-purposes, some fired with wild fantasies, others deadly serious and ready to calculate battle plans, others simply playing the fool. The desire to get things together remained unimpaired, but the means of doing them . . .

At the end of both meetings it was agreed that everyone should come back next week, when the Open Space Committee would be meeting again in closed session. This time we would confront them directly with our demands. Come the day, it was clear the disco campaign was heading for a rebuff. The Committee seemed to have in mind a strictly controlled sport-orientated youth provision, with discos as a faddish side attraction. (One Committee member's half-serious remark when he saw the basement was 'We'll keep these cages in here for the kids who get out of hand'.) Besides, they were already involved in youth provision. Len ran four Sunday League football teams, drawn from the estate.

The kids were angry and confused at the machinations of these people, who wouldn't even let them appear before them to present their case. 'We want the basement for a disco, the rest of the building's theirs, we want a bit of the community centre.'

Finally, led by their most articulate and enthusiastic spokesman, Brian, and some of the Youth Group, they stormed into the Committee meeting-room. They got a hostile reception. Brian was the only one of the kids to speak – and he did so very well. Calmly and rationally he put the case for a disco, and the Committee were obviously surprised and impressed. But this didn't prevent them from answering him with what appeared to be a *non sequitur*. If there was going to be a disco or anything else for youth, it would be available only to those living on the Monmouth. Brian at that time lived on the neighbouring Denby estate.

Despite our eloquent protestations, negotiations were jammed. 'Monmouth facilities are paid for by Monmouth tenants. Denby has its own tenants association and its own tenants' hall, to which Monmouth people aren't invited.'

On this note we finally withdrew from the meeting. It was agreed, however, that the disco issue should be raised for proper discussion at the Committee's next meeting, which we would attend along with Brian and one or two other youngsters.

The Monmouth *v*. Denby controversy was a continuing motif in the story of the Black Horse. Denby is a far older estate; Monmouth people were comparative newcomers. So we can see here the familiar rivalry between the established and outsiders. In many contexts of post-war redevelopment, for example in New Towns, the established have a higher socio-economic status than the outsiders. But here the position was reversed. Many Denby families were poor; the estate contained a lot of pensioners living alone; and a full complement of black families. Living conditions were cramped, and the Council regarded it as something of a problem estate. It had a bad reputation among local police and social workers. In contrast, Monmouth families were relatively better off, if only because many of them were at the stage in their lives with maximum earning power and minimum demands on their incomes. Nevertheless, the sociological differences between the two estates can be over-emphasized. Both, for example, contained many large immigrant families. The critical difference was that the dominant parent culture on Denby was closer to the underclass traditions of the area, whereas on Monmouth the dominant parent culture – as represented by the Open Space Committee – was decidedly respectable and linked with the traditions of trade-union militancy.

The conflict between the two estates was thus an integral effect of the area's history. Now it was being dramatized in a series of incidents which were circulated around the gossip channels on Monmouth. Denby had held a dance and refused to allow Monmouth people; a request by a young girl living on Monmouth to use the Denby tenants' hall for her wedding reception was turned down; and so on. Such incidents were not imaginary: they related to the strategies of social closure (or exclusion) operated by both estates. For example, people of the two estates would not drink in the same pub, and in fact had very little to do with each other.

These adult divisions did not, however, neatly reproduce themselves among the kids. And this posed something of a problem for the adult system of classification. The way they got round it was by using degrees of parental control as indices of status differences among the adults. Monmouth kids were supposed to be polite, well behaved, and nicely dressed, and never to get into trouble. Denby kids were supposed to be dirty, scruffy, noisy, rude and always getting into trouble. On the Monmouth they had it both ways: the Denby kids are like that because of the parents, therefore the parents are like that, and because the parents are like that we don't want to know them – and because we don't want to know them why should we provide things for their kids?

Needless to say no such neat distinctions in behaviour between Monmouth and Denby youngsters could be observed in practice. The Youth Group felt justified in pointing out to the Open Space Committee the irrelevance of the Monmouth *v.* Denby controversy to the issue of the Black Horse disco. To try to exclude Denby youth would be to create divisions where there were none before. But in taking up this position the Group misread the underlying logic of the situation. The issue was not Monmouth *v.* Denby as such, but a conflict of interest between the two different sections of the youth constituency and two different types of provision for them. The conflict existed on both estates. There were the more mainstream youth who were more inclined to accept the dominant parent culture as defining a sense of their possibilities, and the adult discipline of the traditional youth club and football team. And there were the more disaffiliated, who operated more in terms of a street-based culture. Inevitably it was this latter group that the Youth Group had come across and whose needs and demands they had taken up. What confused us was that the Open Space Committee had identified mainstream provision with the Monmouth estate and the disaffiliated kids with Denby. In trying to heal the breach between Monmouth and Denby in the name of youth as a united interest, we unwittingly reinforced the latent division within it. We were seen as publicly siding with the 'unclubbable' youth from both estates against the 'clubbables'. However, given the Youth Group's own place in the political geography, there wasn't very much we could have done about this.

Consequently, at the second meeting of the Open Space Committee the disco lobby was unprepared while the Committee had lost no time organizing a counter-offensive. They had invited some mainstream youth from Monmouth to vindicate the Monmouth Only line.

The most prominent young representative was Kevin, a youth club success and midfield star of Lennie's soccer team. He was also something of a trend-setter. His role as spokesman for official Monmouth youth clearly flattered him, and he delivered his lines about Monmouth Only on cue. The effect on the disparate and in the Committee's eyes unofficial youth was to be shattering.

Most of the disco lobby kowtowed, muffed their lines, or dried up completely. Their acquiescence contrasted sharply with their previous no-holds-barred militancy. Brian alone stood his ground and bravely refused to crumble before this latest manoeuvre. He was deserted, however, by, in his own words, 'people who I thought were my mates'. Some of these happened to live on Monmouth, while Brian lived on Denby. And it was tacitly agreed by all concerned that his views didn't really count. When confronted by 'official' youth, backed by the weight of the parents in a way they weren't, Brian's mates on Monmouth saw which side their bread was buttered. Our attempts to mediate between Kevin and Brian as representatives of the two sides proved abortive. This had been Brian's first real taste of community politics: cliques, deviousness, backstabbing, personal rivalries; he was understandably disillusioned.

As the most articulate and able spokesman for his side, Brian began to identify more and more with us, the Youth Group. He began to prefer the 'intelligent' company of the Group and to look down on his mates as 'stupid, you can't really talk to them, where with you I can say what I think'. This feeling of alienation increased particularly after he was betrayed at the Committee meeting and his mates wouldn't speak to him! The Youth Group felt it was a bad thing to encourage a situation where Brian would be caught in a no-man's-land between us and his mates. The world is cruel to fish out of water, and although it is perhaps illusory to imagine that this could ever be totally successful, the Youth Group decided where possible to pursue a policy of reintegration with your mates. 'You might be cleverer than them, but don't reject them completely, they're the people you were brought up with, they're the people who know you best.'

Thus the series of confrontations we have described had ended in victory for the tenant hardliners and the defeat and disintegration of the kids, not to mention bad feeling between Brian and his mates. Spontaneous enthusiasm just isn't enough to keep the kids together when their position within their own community is polarized politically in this way. The whole problem of young tenants associations, their organizational forms and their relation to the parent organization, is mirrored in the dilemma of Brian and this confrontation of a section of unorganized youth in North London with the Monmouth Open Space Committee.

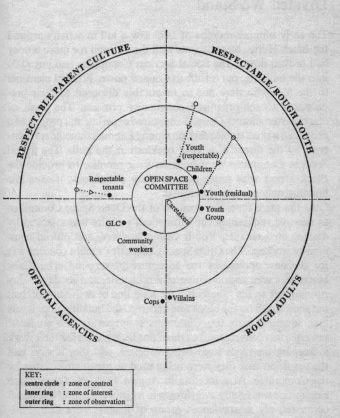

KEY:
centre circle : zone of control
inner ring : zone of interest
outer ring : zone of observation

Black Horse: Confrontation over disco (May 1973).

Divided We Stand

The early summer months of 1973 saw a lull in activity around the Black Horse. Negotiations with the Council for more money had broken down. The Social Services Committee had put £800 into the building, but a shift in Council power brought elements to the fore who were not so favourably disposed as their predecessors to self-organized community projects. The wave of scandal over another Council-supported experimental project had provoked a predictable reaction among Labour councillors frightened by the threat of a Tory backlash at the polls. The Social Services Committee went back on their promise to provide the Black Horse with more money. They pulled out, leaving the building only partially renovated.

At the same time, the position of the Open Space Committee as the sole spokesman for Monmouth's affairs was attacked by discontented tenants, Youth Group workers, and official community workers. The Open Space Committee's main concern was for the development of the adventure playground. The Black Horse was seen as something of a millstone, and its day-to-day running left to the 'students', the long line of activists who had put their heads on the block and occupied the building since it was first squatted with the Committee's approval. The students' presence was convenient, but there was little thanks for their work in keeping the place from being wrecked, and they always had the suspicion that they were being used as expendable dupes by the Committee. At a meeting in August 1973, the Open Space Committee was finally overthrown in a bitter coup, and a new and comparatively inexperienced group of tenants were democratically elected as the official Tenants Association. This was done with not a little prodding from local Community Organizer, Gerry Stern, a young man working for the Home-Office-backed Community Development Commission.

The setting-up of the Monmouth Tenants Association signalled an irreconcilable split between them and the Open Space Committee, which from then on had to confine its activities to playspace. The Tenants Association was meanwhile carefully nursed by Stern. Its task was to provide a forum for tenants' complaints, which could then be channelled through to relevant GLC departments, and to represent the tenants in negotiations with the Black Horse's owners – again the GLC.

The new Tenants Association Committee faced a basic problem shared by all tenants associations; that involved in fostering and maintaining a liaison with the mass of the tenants on the one hand and with the 'authorities' on the other. This dual role means that tenants association committees must face in two directions at once: they are placed squarely in the middle and exposed to the possibility of being caught in the cross-fire between the two warring factions. A tenant association committee gains its identity and effectiveness through the extent to which it can build a realistic relationship with the two sides. In the case of the authorities, it is either confrontative or collusive. The other relationship of the tenants association committee – that with the mass of tenants whom it represents – is even less fixed and stable. What is the role of the Committee member? Is he representative, delegate, servant? The whole gamut of attitudes were displayed towards Committee members on the Monmouth – everything from deference and respect, through 'the person who can help me with my problems', to 'mug who does the dirty work'. Any tenants association committee must carve out a role and identity for itself by delicate 'negotiation' with its grass roots support. What a task! Divided they stand . . .

The new Committee was subjected to intense socialization into the rituals of organization by Stern. The Tenants Liaison Officer from the local Council also came down and gave what amounted to a lecture on committee procedure. The finer points of the quorum, the metaphysics of minute taking, the divine right of chairmanship – this to an audience composed of a bus conductor, a taxi driver, a milkman, and three housewives. Perhaps for the first time since they had left school, they were presented with a model of how to behave – a behaviourism in which they recognized the subjection of their own culture, but found an apparent means of mastering their environment. If they could learn the ropes, they could handle the GLC – and this, in turn, would increase their standing among the tenants.

So there was one of the housewives putting up her hand to ask about points of order; there was the milkman asking how motions were passed – exercises in painful deference to learning. In the long run, to master the three Rs of the constitution, to defer and refer to it, is also supposed to extract a proper deference from the rank and file. So it is all too easy for a tenants association committee like this to end up acting in the name of the constitution. After all, acting in the name of the people they 'represent' isn't as easy as it sounds. What *are* the wishes of the tenants? Do they agree on anything? Surreptitiously the constitution becomes the Committee's authority when their representative role is called into question, when things threaten to get out of hand. The trouble in this case was that living on the Monmouth was to experience things continually getting out of hand. Broken windows, street fights, squatters round the corner, family disputes . . . On this new mass estate, where there were no institutions of social control intrinsic to the culture, where rumour had taken over the function of gossip, the level of anxiety was enormously high. Of course this prevailing sense of anxiety gave the Tenants Association one of its reasons for existence – but they needed to armour themselves against the subversive and seductive powers of that anxiety. This was the symbolic function of the constitution perhaps – a magical device providing just such an armour.

The conscious performance of the constitution, especially before any kind of audience, unfortunately reinforced the very anxiety it was supposed to dispel. Meetings would grate through long stretches of boredom procedure, interspersed with violent outbursts of aggression, rumour, sexual innuendo – moments when the culture and the anxieties it contained burst through, only to be eventually stifled by the call to order and the panacea of boredom.

While the Tenants Association Committee was suffering its birth pangs, the Youth Group was faced with the possibility of encouraging youth militancy around the issue of a disco club for the Black Horse pub. It will be remembered that the haphazard youth alliance had suffered a heavy defeat at the hands of the Open Space Committee. Subsequently, there had been talk of storming the place and occupying it, with vague threats from some boys of putting the place out of commission if they weren't given what they wanted. However, direct action was rejected by the Youth Group – why march yet another youth army up yet another futile hill?

So with the demise of the Open Space Committee and the ascendance of the new Tenants Association, the Youth Group decided to embark on the tactics of careful patient negotiation.

Because of the Youth Group's limited resources, close involvement with the Tenants Association meant a consequent relaxation of involvement with the kids. There followed in the late summer months an interminable series of attendances at meetings, keeping a diplomatic and responsible profile, until the issue of the disco was raised, invariably at the fag end of the agenda. This tactic of progress through negotiation did have some important advantages, however. The presence of the Youth Group as a group began to register on the tenants, and to its proposals was lent a credibility which perhaps was not there before. Who were we? What right did we have to speak (as opposed to simply volunteering to do the shitwork)? Now these doubts were hardly raised except in anger. The relationship of the Youth Group and the disco project to the Tenants Association was legitimized.

This recognition of the disco project by the Committee was somewhat grudging, though. Indeed, Committee members diverged in their attitudes. In contrast to the vacillations of his colleagues, Archie Jones was the strongest supporter.

Archie was something of a misfit on the Committee. He was the only member who didn't have a totally respectable past. His dad was a bookie. Born in Bermondsey, he had grown up very much part of the petty criminal milieu of the area. More than his colleagues, he had knocked around as a young man. He had worked in night-clubs and casinos in the West End, and had been around the disco and club scene of the rhythm and blues era, as had his wife. All this he brought to a vision of the Black Horse which was much closer to the Youth Group's ideas, and was also shared by the younger members of the Committee. He saw this future community centre as a promotional venture – smart, sophisticated, young orientated, perhaps a bit like the ritzy working men's clubs of the North – a members' bar, a cabaret, intimate lighting, the odd private film show.

Archie was a lone hustler – by far the most competent (at moments, inspired) member of the Committee in the complex game of negotiation, bluff and counter-bluff with the GLC, yet quite incapable of presenting himself or his achievements to the tenants in a manner which would gain their respect and approval. Archie was seen as 'a bit fly', 'flash'. He went out of his way to restrict his role on the Committee to negotiating with the GLC and tried to have as little contact with his constituency as possible. When the chairmanship of the Committee became vacant, the Youth Group encouraged him to take on the job (which was his for the asking). He refused. He preferred to operate quietly behind the scenes, leaving others to face the tenants. Unlike the rest of the Committee, he even refused to collect subscriptions from his block on behalf of the Tenants Association.

Concerned solely with negotiations with the GLC, Archie was involved with only one side of the Committee's functions. He persuaded the rest of the Committee that their strongest card in negotiations both for the building and for the funds to run it was to demonstrate to the authorities in some tangible form the need for the building. This was what the disco represented.

The Monmouth Tenants Association Committee was caught in a dilemma. As a pressure group, to force the Council to 'get things done' they had to an extent to start things off themselves. To prove to the Council the need for a community centre, they had to put their skills as plumbers, builders, community organizers, on the line. But the Committee members didn't necessarily see that as part of their brief. So whose job was it? Obviously, they thought, the Youth Group's. But we made it clear that we weren't there to run the whole show. It would have to be the disco or nothing.

Consequently the disco became identified with the Black Horse and the Black Horse with the disco. But this didn't mean that the tenants' attitudes to the youth had undergone any real change. Indeed it may actually have hardened existing attitudes. This ambivalence towards the disco was illustrated when, in the course of a long diatribe by the Committee against the kids and their disco, one of the Youth Group asked them point black, 'Do you want it closed down then?', and got the reply, 'Oh no, there'd be nothing going on at all here then'.

One positive outcome of these developments was that a Youth Group member was seconded on to the Committee (later he also took on the production of the Tenants Newsletter); while Archie Jones was delegated to oversee the disco.

Archie's twin involvements with the disco and the GLC effectively sealed him off from the pressure of prejudiced opinion on the estate – Monmouth people, who as we have shown, already disapproved of rough 'Denby-type' kids, would soon find a focal-point for their resentment in the Black Horse disco. This was not Archie's concern, but was more worrying to those Committee members with their ears closest to the ground: the housewives. Throughout its history, the level of resentment against the disco among Committee members rose in direction proportion to their proximity to grass roots opinion (channelled through the housewives), and in inverse proportion to their proximity to negotiations with the GLC (channelled through Archie, the chairman, and so on). Needless to say, it would have been unthinkable for the housewives on the Committee to extend their role beyond anything more than collecting subscriptions and providing a crude sounding-board for the latest rumours and panics about 'rough' kids and deteriorating conditions on the estate.

This is not an unusual set up. The average age of tenants committees in London is 49·7 years, and 68·5 per cent of the members are married women. So most tenants associations tend to be dominated by women who may have half a lifetime of frustration as housewives behind them . . . and this could be another driving force behind many of the intransigent positions they take up. The Tenants Association on the Monmouth may have felt at times no more than a working-class version of a Hampstead amenity group, but one thing we have to remember is that the first concerns of housebound mums are the conditions on the estate where they spend all their days, and the second, the concern to prevent the kids running wild. On a spick and span new estate, some quickly become ardent conservationists – they want to take a broom and duster to the landing and a broom-handle to the kids – and these women tend to get active in the tenants associations. For others, pride in the place stops at their own front door.

In the Monmouth Tenants Association, no one but a man could have held the chairman's job. In this way, the division of labour in the working-class household, reproduced itself in the power relationships within the Committee. Trouble with the kids or with neighbours? 'Wait till my husband/your father gets home!' Noise from the disco? 'My Charlie's on the Committee, he'll sort that out.' The women agitate, the men are supposed to ameliorate, and they didn't always feel comfortable doing that! In the workplace, backed by a hundred years of male trade-unionism, these men are confident enough in their dealings with officialdom; but when it comes to the state of the drains, repairs on the estate, and the alleged teenage rampage, these militants suddenly become ill at ease. They often felt plain silly talking with local government representatives about these kinds of problems. The implications of all this for the women's movement, which has done hardly any work in this area, should be obvious.

As for the tenants movement as a whole, the fact has to be faced that the majority of tenants associations remain confined to a consumer model dominated by the housewife interest at the level of both action and consciousness. The Monmouth Tenants Association was brought together while the struggle against the Housing Finance Act and the Industrial Relations Act was at its height and the mineworkers forced a General Election and the defeat of the Tory government. Yet outside occupational communities – Clay Cross, Merthyr Tydfil, Merseyside, etc. – the tenants movement was frankly overshadowed by the trade unions when it came to confronting the Tory offensive. It's hard even to think of fighting class legislation when you're bogged down in a welter of drains that don't work, inadequate street lighting, and nowhere for the kids to play. On the Monmouth, the Youth Group tried on several occasions to raise the wider political issues, to make the connections. Perhaps when the miners came into King's Cross Station, the Tenants Association could offer them the facilities of the pub as it was just down the road? All this produced was an embarrassed silence. After all, what had the miners' struggle to do with them? The Association chairman, an active trade-unionist and member of the local Labour Party, would constantly remind the Youth Group with a wry smile that the Tenants Association is 'non-political, remember'. Politics, like religion, was something decided among consenting adults in the privacy of their own home.

There are obviously profound historical reasons for such attitudes. In the case of the Monmouth Tenants Association the latent conservatism would at least have been shaken up by the recruitment of individuals who could balance the demands of a relationship with the tenants on the one hand and with the authorities on the other. This would have made the Association more effective. Greater effectiveness, and a way through the impasse of the kind of ideology imposed on Committee organization, may well be necessary preconditions for making a tenants association a political force – both in its own neighbourhood and as part of the working-class movement. However, they are certainly not sufficient.

Whatever Happened to the Teenage Dream?

By the beginning of the autumn, the Youth Group's careful negotiations with the Tenants Association and the Area Youth Office finally began to bear fruit. A date was fixed for the opening

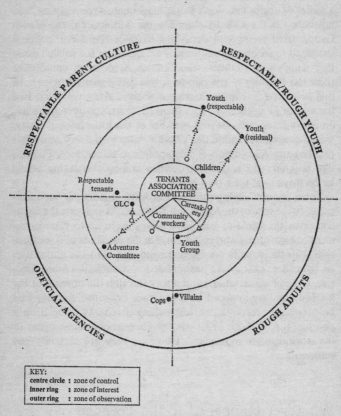

KEY:
centre circle : zone of control
inner ring : zone of interest
outer ring : zone of observation

Black Horse: circa birth of Monmouth Tenants Association and overthrow of Open Space Committee (August 1973).

of the senior disco, and the Youth Group could now deliver the good news to their constituency. The kids, especially those who had been involved first time round, were both surprised and cynical. 'We'll believe it when we see it.' From their point of view the whole thing must have had the appearance of a conjuring trick. The disco was simply being produced out of thin air, and the whole process that had gone into producing it (the careful negotiations) was invisible to them.

In the kids' eyes, this only reinforced the ambiguity of the Youth Group's position. 'Who are they?' 'What are they doing it for?' First of all the kids tried to place us in institutional categories – for example, teacher, youth worker. This may have been our objective status, but simply didn't tally with the context in which we were working or with our style of operating. We didn't try to be 'one of the boys'. So then subcultural categories were tried – student, hippy. That one lasted a bit longer; after all there were plenty of those about. But eventually it too was rejected. The Group's image was too 'hard' for that. Finally, there was only one category left which fitted with the way the Group was seen to operate in relation to the authorities. 'They must be hustlers.' Such a definition, although a mark of some respect and acceptance (and perhaps it was nearer the truth than the other labels!), also posed certain problems. Hustlers don't do something for nothing, and where was the pay-off in all this? It was obvious that the disco was being set up on a shoestring, and no one was making anything out of it, and yet hustlers was the nearest they could get . . .

On one occasion, though, one of the regulars put it this way: 'You're educated, but you don't talk educated, you've sort of come out of your class, you're in between, you're trying to help us, but you're not one of us . . . But you don't want us to be like you either . . . You must be mad!'

The Junior Disco

At the same time as the senior disco was being prepared, a junior disco was opened for the 5–14 age group – again in response to the kids' insistent demands; and with the adventure playground still pretty much a bomb site, their need was urgent enough. As their spokesmen pointed out, the Black Horse had after all been originally their den. And they weren't going to be left out of the reckoning now. If they were, well there wouldn't be much of the building left standing for anyone else to use!

The way the younger kids pressed home their demands was encouraging, but it concealed a problem. Just as the teenagers had demanded a disco, because somehow that was what they were expected to want, so the younger kids demanded their own version of the same – because they were expected to imitate their elders.

Wanting to be like older brothers and sisters, or their friends, is institutionalized in the kind of age group system we're describing. But this picture was complicated by a particular mutation in the system that was taking place at this time. Girls in the 8–14 age group were increasingly rejecting their role as child-minders; they were breaking away to form their own distinctive peer group, parallel to, but independent from the boys'.

This development was undoubtedly the effect of wider changes in the political economy of the working-class household, changes which had disturbed the traditional system of rights and obligations between wage-earning and wageless members. On the Monmouth more mothers were going out to work and male bread-winners were being pressed into 'domestic service'. And as the sexual division of labour became more fluid and negotiable, so too did the division of labour between the generations. One effect of this was to intensify rivalries inside some families – between brothers and sisters, younger and older kids. One thirteen-year-old girl has put it like this:

My little sister who is five years old
Spends her life making mine a misery
According to Mum she does everything she's told,
But not where I am concerned.
For I must not take her things, she's not supposed to take mine
Although she does
I argue and say I want them back.

50

'Oh no,' says mum, 'you shouldn't fight
after all Nicola is only five and you're thirteen.'
I make the beds, and do the washing up,
I go to the shops but I don't get any thanks.
'Mind the wet floor, hang up your coat.'
It wasn't like this before Nicola came.

And one resolution of this dilemma was the creation of a new peer group of pre-adolescent girls, *outside* the family, as a new stage in their life-cycle.

On the positive side, it meant a rejection, however unconscious, of the whole process of anticipatory socialization into their role as 'household mums'. On the negative side, the only vehicle of expression these girls had was the established forms of the contemporary youth spectacle. So the self-discovery of this new sub-generation became simply their assertion of an age-specific presence as consumers within a commercial pop culture which had been previously reserved exclusively for their teenage brothers and sisters.

It was the emergence of this new peer-group generation of working-class girls which provided the mass social base for 'Osmond-mania', which was at that time sweeping the country. But pop groups like the Osmonds, the Jackson Five, David Cassidy, however skilfully they may have exploited the phenomenon, did not create it. If they were successful it was because their fans – almost exclusively girls in the 8–14 age group – *recognized* themselves in the pre-adolescent persona of their heroes, especially in their domesticated, pre-genital sexuality. The bigger his following, the bigger little Donny Osmond grew in the grown-up world of entertainment, and by association the bigger, the more grown-up his child fans could feel in their own eyes. It was by shrewdly manipulating this basic polarity of childhood (big/little)* in the name of its imaginary emancipation that Osmond-mania produced in these kids a *mis-recognition* of their real situation. The rejection of childhood as apprenticeship for

---

* Big/little is a polarity of the child's pre-oedipal fantasy world which anticipates and prestructures the later male/female poles of identity and difference.

motherhood, their rights and needs as an interest group in their own neighbourhoods, all that was successfully repressed from consciousness, subsumed in the hysteria of the live concerts, the fan mags and the rest, where suddenly, 'as if by magic', this sub-generation was present to itself for the first time.

So the demand for a junior disco was more complex than it first appeared. In fact it concealed two, distinctly antagonistic de-mands: the girls wanted to start a local chapter of the Donny Osmond Fan Club; the boys wanted a cross between an indoor adventure playground and the North Bank terrace at Arsenal. So when the doors were opened, the organizers found they had *two* distinct clubs which just happened to coincide at the one time and place. The boys swarmed all over the place, swung from the lights, held races across tables and chairs, savaged the football machine and had impromptu bundle fights on the floors, all this interspersed with much North Bank football chanting. They came in scruffy and came out looking – as one mum put it – 'like they've been out in a spin dryer'.

But the girls . . . ! Dressed to the nines in their best party clothes, and the latest teen fashion. Here and there a hint of eye shadow and deft application of mum's Chanel No. 5. At the first bars of 'Long Haired Lover' they 'took' the dance floor, and remained there for the rest of the evening as if hypnotized, impervious to the boys' bedlam; ten-year-old seductive swaying bottoms, rolling hips – a completely convincing imitation of teen-age discosex. Mostly, the boys ignored them, but from time to time, the chant would go up from the North Bank: 'Donny's a poofta, Donny's a poofta.'* To which the girls would inevitably chorus, 'Charlie's a wanker' (i.e. Charlie George, the footballer).

Billy Sheahan (see page 22) would frequently pay a visit:

---

* Osmond-baiting was in fact one of the most familiar weapons used by older brothers in their continuous bickering with their younger sisters. A fourteen-year-old boy told how 'we went by the Rainbow [Theatre] once and we started screaming out the window, "Osmonds are bent, all queers", and they were lobbing everything that come in sight. You see one of them, she's in a state crying over the railing going "you bastards" and the next minute she picked up a bottle and threw it at the bus.'

the C.O. come to inspect his troops and make sure they are having a good time. He would stroll around, chatting to his mates, offering the especially-favoured fags (Billy always smoked the most expensive brands). He would never condescend to join in the proceedings – 'all that's kid's stuff'. And so he'd wander off again into the night, 'got to attend to business, ta ta', an eleven-year-old miniature adult with two middle-aged kids as parents to support.

Some of the organizers tried to find ways of enlarging the scope of the junior disco, to develop activities which would bring the boys' and girls' groups into some kind of positive relation, be geared to their own stage of development and give them back a sense of themselves as an autonomous interest group. But they found that once the situation had been publicly defined as a 'disco' it was well-nigh impossible to change or extend it.

At the least, the junior disco provided an opportunity to involve local parents in the Black Horse. Local mums were asked to come along to help out, and a few came. At first they were scandalized by the goings-on – especially by the boys' behaviour. Unfortunately – and coincidentally – most of the boys came from Denby, while most of the girls came from Monmouth. So the disco served only as further confirmation of their views on the relative status of the two estates! At first the new helpers resorted to the tried and tested strategies of parental control to keep order. Threats of a clout, and the actual thing. Perhaps for the first time, it didn't work. They were met with derision or open retaliation; and they were after all outnumbered, twenty to one. And then they began to relax, the mums especially, to stand back, and to intervene only where things were really getting out of hand and someone was likely to get hurt. This perhaps was the one positive success that the junior disco did manage to achieve in its short history.

With the junior disco under way, and the senior disco about to open, the Youth Group, badly overstretched, tried to enlist the help and support of 'revolutionary' socialist organizations in the area, but 'the comrades' showed little interest in working with teenagers; they were only interested in whether they could sell their newspapers around the estate. The Group then turned to the student community activists. They were predictably keen to work with kids but retreated from the edge of militancy that seemed to accompany the work.

A comic attempt to 'win' local youth 'to socialism' was in fact made during this period by a Trotskyist group, then known as the Socialist Labour League. Some boys from Highbury arrived at the disco one evening, and remarked that they had been accosted in Chapel Market: 'This geezer comes up to us and starts talking about the revolution and all this, and how they've got this disco club, it's just opened but they got no members, so would we like to go . . . And we told 'im to piss off, 'cos I mean why would we go down there, we've already got a place [the Black Horse], it's more like your own place, innit?'

After the initial success of the opening night, when some 120 people – mainly between the ages of fourteen and seventeen, free schoolers, young black kids, exiles, loners – came to 'suss out' the scene, the ranks of the small core group who had helped get the pub ready were swelled, especially by girls. Through the local network, a young black disco team came in to provide the sounds.* On a total budget of £100, the ground floor of the pub had been kitted out with all the essential props of a commercial disco. A light show, pop art dance floor, a bar area, and intimate lighting. Most of the gear had been begged, borrowed, or stolen, but the smart image prevailed, and the Youth Group did what they could to emphasize it. Some care was taken in the presentation of the evening to give it a distinctly West End gloss.

In the early weeks, a pattern of activity soon emerged. The girls would arrive early and more or less take over the dance floor for the first half of the evening; they were particularly good at formation dancing. The regular lads would drop in, pay their entrance, nip over to the pub across the road, to return, suitably tanked up, for the latter part of the evening.

* Although few black girls attended the disco throughout its history, and the black boys were very popular with the white girls, there was never any suggestion of racial tension.

Accordingly, the Youth Group divided its labours between the disco and the pub. (It's impossible to hear yourself talk in a disco.) Recognizing the need for the lads to have a few drinks before getting up the courage to be seen dancing in public with girls, the Group listened with some sympathy to pleas to relax the No Alcohol rule. In practice, they turned a blind eye to booze on the premises, within reason.

A successful evening – lights turned down low, a pleasant haze of smoke and alcohol, couples cheek to cheek on the dance floor, the slow gossip to the door. But it wasn't always like that. Often the atmosphere would become brittle – the noise of the disco could barely camouflage the boredom and sexual anxiety of the members. It was the difference between a Sense of Occasion and Desolation Row.

Such sudden changes in mood and membership are a common experience to club managers, both commercial and youth service. Often they seem to happen for no apparent reason. Is there any logic behind them? Why do kids go to discos? To get off the street, and meet others of the same age – and different sex. That's obvious enough. But they also go looking for new faces, new talent – to break out from the restricted social networks based on the street and neighbourhood. Initially they go with their mates. What these simple facts conceal is the complicated way in which the painful transitional process from being one of the lads or lasses to being a couple takes place. We will show later how the territorial rules of affinity and enmity both codify the ambiguities of distance intrinsic to this transition, and lock the whole thing in to local group boundaries. To visit a city centre disco is to be on neutral territory, to subordinate temporarily these rigid in-group, out-group rules to a more open pick-up system, where everything is negotiable and open to the chance encounter: mystery boy meets mystery girl like strangers in the night. It's a safe way of shedding the protective identity of the group, which is still there if you need it.

The problem with locality-based discos like the Black Horse is that, however hard one tries to create West End atmosphere and the sense of occasion that goes with it, the very urban context in which one is working militates against it. Kids might come at first looking for a more open-ended scene, soon to find only the same old faces. In some cases where this happens, out of the sense of weekly anti-climax, the kids create their own negative sense of occasion – fights, smashing up, the revival and settling of old scores. In other cases, as in the Black Horse, where the pattern of affinity and enmity has lost its territorial function and the social network has become attenuated, the response can be more internalized. When there aren't any enemies, or outsiders, and not much sense of affinity, then the kids are just left face to face with each other and themselves. The real social nightmare breaks through: the ambiguities of relationships between boys and girls and within their respective peer groups come to the surface.

After the first big opening night at the Black Horse, membership began to fall off – fewer people each week attracted fewer people the next. The Youth Group tried desperately to reverse this process by improvising a Sense of Occasion. Dance competitions, raffles, a Christmas party with a live band. The success of the band raised the demand, especially from the boys, to have a live band every week. So live music came to the Black Horse, and once again membership snowballed.

The regular core of girls were less enthusiastic about this development. The music of many of the groups was more suitable for listening to than for dancing to. Formation dancing is its own live performance, and the arrival of the musicians threaded to steal the show. Sometimes there were even requests from the girls to 'turn them off' or 'put another one on', just like a record. Girls also tended to be more 'Top of the Pops' orientated, while many of the boys aspired to more sophisticated tastes – progressive, reggae, and rhythm and blues.

But above all the boys tended to appreciate more fully than the girls the aspect of *performance* that the bands brought to the Black Horse. Many identified directly with the 'macho' pose and stance of the young musicians; there was never any shortage of volunteers to help set up the electronic hardware. On one occasion, however, the musicians tried to exploit the situation by exhortations from the stage to 'get it on' and strip off! The kids' response to this subcultural attack was to close ranks and drown out the band in a chorus of repartee. The band had seriously misread the expectations of their audience. Taking the repartee for personal insult they got increasingly uncomfortable and finally stalked off the stage.

On bad nights, particularly before the advent of the groups, there seemed little that could be done to lift the place out of its depression. Moreover it was precisely at these low ebb moments that the more isolated and disturbed kids came into their own – they struck home. One particular boy, Kelly, had a habit of walking up and down the floor, through the dispirited ranks of huddled teenagers, and choosing a victim; he would slap him or her violently on the back in a gesture of simulated friendliness; the victim would be sent flying across the floor, while Kelly would just stand grinning. Another boy, Neil, broke a leg off a chair one time, and beat it on the table violently in time to the music. This acting-out of personal anxieties and alienations was never the prelude to fights or smashing up. The other kids somehow recognized disturbed behaviour for what it was and simply tended to avoid it like the emotional plague.

One evening Kelly, in a particularly disruptive mood, goaded a group of exiles from Highbury, who to their credit ignored him. In a group situation such a challenge would have been taken up according to the affinity/enmity code. But Kelly was on his own, and these lads knew they had a nutter on their hands. Kelly, forced to follow through, pursued the boys to where they had chosen to sit together and accidentally on purpose whipped the chair away from underneath one of them. He got the chair back in his face for his pains. Rather than this developing into a generalized scuffle between the newcomers and the home crew, everybody seemed more concerned to protect Kelly from himself.

Indeed, kids are often better at dealing with such sources of disturbance than their adult supervisors. Contrast this episode with another which occurred round about the same time. A small group from the Black Horse had been visiting another club and had made a desultory attempt to take it over. The inevitable sequence of insult, challenge and fight had duly taken place, and the following week the feud was carried back to the Black Horse. But at the moment of showdown the Black Horse boys conspicuously failed to get a crew up and gratefully handed the matter over to the cops. As one of the boys described it:

There was going to be a big fight. Sixty of them came down, all ready to steam in with chains, iron bars, all that. Well, someone (one of the boys) give a tip to the old bill and they've come down in meat wagons and rovers and they're all hiding in the back and when this copper shouts 'now', they've all rushed out and caught as many as they can and they've frisked them all down and got all their tools off them 'n' that, and they've took them up the old bill and they're nicked, aren't they? They've had it then.'

It quickly became clear that the disco evening alone would never generate a group solidarity among the kids as an interest group in the area. In a way the disco was simply reinforcing the social nightmare through its atmospherics.

'I Wanna Be Your Boyfriend'

One positive side to this period: the Youth Group got to understand something of the personal relationships that were going on under the surface of 'the scene'. For instance, there was Neil and his Valentine . . .

Neil was in love with Ellen, a leading member of the girls' 'formation dance set' in the disco. Ellen was very popular among the girls – she was always surrounded by her mates; but she was less often seen with a boy. The boys had, of course, classified all the girls into the familiar two categories: the slags who'd go with anyone and everyone (they were all right for a quick screw, but you'd never get serious about it) and the drags who didn't but whom you might one day think about going steady with. Needless to say, different cliques of boys put different girls in each of the two categories, and there was often a good deal of argument about the status to be accorded to particular girls. There was a consensus, however, about Ellen: you couldn't get near her.

Neil was transfixed. He was sure it was the Real Thing. He'd bought Ellen birthday and Christmas presents, which she'd acknowledged but no more. So then he bought her a Valentine – the biggest and most luxurious money could buy.

However, Ellen continued to pointedly ignore him in the disco. Finally, in desperation, he canvassed our services as go-betweens. Tactfully to put in a word? No, that was breaking an unwritten law of this particular code: never talk to your mates about a girl when you're serious. Perhaps he should offer to take her out, say to the ice rink, making it clear that he wasn't after anything more than her company? The suggestion plunged Neil into agonies of doubt. He no more dared ask her out than confide his feelings on the matter to his mates. He was caught. If he took her out and didn't make up to her, she might think he was 'slow' or, worse, that there was 'something wrong' with him. On the other hand, if he did make advances, he might just get his face slapped – and then Ellen might put the word around and he'd be shown up to all his mates.

Ellen was caught in a parallel bind. She was popular with her mates, but one attribute of popularity was having a boyfriend, at least to talk about. On the other hand, she knew Neil was 'serious', otherwise he would have invited her out by now. (Although, as we've seen, Neil didn't know that she knew he was serious, and Ellen didn't know he didn't know.) But Ellen wasn't ready for a 'serious' relationship, she was too young to start going steady. Then again, she'd be 'safe' with Neil, she could string him along while she made up her mind what to do. She wouldn't be safe with a pick-up. That would be less complicated emotionally, but then if she let the boy have it, there might be other unwanted complications! And he might put the word around among his mates and she'd be put into the slag bag. And she didn't want that.

The rules of this game revolve around defining ambiguities of distance and relation. What is 'going steady'? When is it 'serious'? Does it depend on how long you spend together at any one time? Or on how regularly you go out? How much is 'regularly'? Does it count if you go out in company with friends? Or does it have to be just the two of you? Is going to the disco together as serious as going to the cinema with friends? Does it make a difference if the cinema is in the West End rather than local? And so on and so forth. And finally all this leads to the basic question: 'What is the meaning attached to doing it, or not doing it?' Most of these rules are arbitrated by the boys' peer group. But there may be inconsistencies between different groups. Or the rules may be applied inconsistently for a particular boy. All this is fiercely talked over in the girls' own group.

Given these interlocking binds, and the complementary dual moralities which generate them, it's a miracle that these kids didn't tie themselves into knots more often than they did. It's hardly surprising that few if any of these boys and girls will ever manage to establish a durable working relationship with each other, outside the two extremes of the perfunctory late-night screw down by Regents Canal or at a mate's party, and the life-long devotions of marriage and having a family.

A few of the Black Horse kids had more officially recognized 'problems'. There was the thirteen-year-old girl, one of the regulars, who kept 'running away from home' and ended up usually spending the night with one of the boys she met at the disco. She would then go home and tearfully spill the beans to mum. This created problems, not just for the Youth Group but, of course, for the boys: police investigations, possible charges of under-age sex. Just why this girl wanted to leave home became apparent one night when her mum, a stout Irish lady, turned up and dragged her out of the disco literally by her hair, to an accompaniment of slaps, punches, and accusations that the place was little better than a brothel and she'd have it closed down!

More seriously, there was Phil MacIlroy. The MacIlroy family had the dubious honour of being No. 1 problem family in the borough. They had certainly had more caseworkers caseworking them for more time, individually and collectively, than any other family in the area.

Mr MacIlroy had been, in his prime, a famous fighting drunk in the Irish community. But too many fights and too many drinks had taken their toll. He had had a stroke, and now had lost the use of his voice and of his left arm. Phil strongly identified with his old man, but now all he could see was a pathetic cripple. At sixteen, he had to take his place as head of a very large and unruly household. His mum, who had held the family together in traditional fashion for so long, had finally cracked under the strain. Large doses of valium weren't enough to keep her from blowing up in screaming fits of rage, or attempting suicide. She was periodically taken into hospital. There were four other children in the family. The eldest sister was eighteen, and extremely 'butch'. She now fought Phil for the man's role in the house, quite literally, with her fists – and Phil's face showed the marks. While the eldest son and daughter were re-enacting the parental scenario of twenty years before, the younger kids were all but totally neglected. They never went to school unless dragged there by a social worker, and were continuously getting into trouble with the law.

To get away from this chronic family crisis, Phil naturally spent as much time outside as he could. Sometimes with a few mates. Other times he would sit and drink by himself in the Cross Keys. He was clearly troubled, as he had every right to be. He was trapped between being Phil and being a MacIlroy, two poles of an identity which negated each other, and which threatened to pull him apart. But he had a lot of resilience; he was doing a precarious balancing act, and at the time the Youth Group knew him, he was pulling it off.

One thing was certain: all the caseworkers in the world wouldn't put the MacIlroy family back together again. But they could still succeed in making things even worse. Perhaps as an admission of this professional failure, the MacIlroy family were offered *in toto* to the cause of science. They were wheeled out one night in a TV programme about 'problem' families. There, before millions of viewers, and their own neighbours, the agony of a London Irish family was dispassionately dissected by a behavioural scientist. No doubt they were paid a fee and told that their case might help others in similar circumstances.

In none of these contexts did we feel we had the right to intervene. The Youth Group was there to help run the disco. What happened outside that, in our own lives, or the kids', was none of the others' concern. This was a deliberate policy. For by structuring the relationship in this way, we at least opened up a clearly defined space which could be filled by real emotions shared by both partners to the deal: like, dislike, mutual interests or disinterests, even mutual aid. For instance, on one occasion two members of the Youth Group had a row in the Cross Keys. Tempers flared and it nearly came to blows; but one of the Tenants Committee (Archie Jones) intervened on one side and one of the disco regulars (Phil MacIlroy) intervened on the other. Both of them recognized it for what it was – a row between best mates familiar enough in their own lives. The best mates forgave each other, and the incident was quickly forgotten. A few weeks later, these same two members of the Youth Group had to perform a similar support function for two of the kids who had fallen out.

Now all this may go against the textbook. But better, surely, to work this way than to adopt the phoney 'niceness' and the yes yes No. 3 smile which characterizes the professional armoury of the traditional social worker. Still less the collusive sharing of 'personal problems', the mutual eliciting of confidences which goes under the banner of 'progressive' technique, but goes against the whole grain of working-class relationships. Not that we think our response to the emotional problems of some of the kids was anything less than inadequate. The issue of creating the forms of a genuine mass therapy, which is organic to the situation of working-class youth and can tackle the impasses of their inner lives, remains wide open. Wilhelm Reich may have posed the question in the thirties, but he was concerned only with its external aspects – sex education, and so on. The question remains to be answered.

On one particularly low-ebb evening of the Black Horse disco, the Youth Group took an initiative and stopped the disco, explaining that the time had come to decide about its future. Immediately the music stopped the kids came alive (some fifty of them), and a lively, if chaotic, meeting took place, everyone talking and shouting and laughing at once.

Whatever Happened to the Teenage Dream?

This spontaneously organized meeting was to prove the first of a general pattern of 'meetings about the disco' and other related matters (for example, a proposed newsletter). Announced in advance by the Youth Group, they took place at varying intervals, usually in an evening, though Sunday afternoon was touted around as a good time when later on the demand for the the place to be open Saturday *and* Sunday grew. It was always hard to predict who would actually show up at these meetings (as opposed to who said they would), and they were often badly handled by the Youth Group, who, because of the strain on their time and resources, and the confusion of the situation surrounding the Black Horse generally, were often unable to give a clear line, and were sometimes as unsure as the kids what they wanted. (The general lesson appears to be: never call a meeting unless you know in advance what you want out of it.) The personnel at these meetings would consist largely of one or other friendship group, or clique. The greater the group solidarity, the more supportive and secure the atmosphere, the more pointed and purposeful the meeting.

Perhaps the most fruitful meeting was with a group of boys from Highbury who had a clear sense of their own collective identity (they were outsiders in the area and were, in a sense, homeless, looking for an operational base of their own). These lads backed each other up and thus helped ensure the credibility of each contribution. In contrast the more loose-knit and haphazard alignments of the home team based around the Black Horse produced a different picture. Rather than backing each other up, everybody would be talking at cross-purposes and at once – unless someone had a riveting or amusing story to tell which commanded the attention of the whole audience.

Meetings would also often be dominated by an ongoing sexual divisiveness. But the flirtations, rivalries, chauvinistic poses, exhibitionism and sexual provocativeness generally, in fact, marked a serious refusal by the boys to take anything the girls said seriously. This, in spite of the obvious capability of the girls to make sensible proposals for action and the encouragement given to them by the Youth Group.

The Fall of the Black Horse Disco

Finally, of course, there was the problem of the disruptive elements, some of whom had begun to have an alarmingly over-developed sense of identity with the place. Invariably a minority of one or two, they tend to see meetings where everybody decides things together as some kind of personal threat and to take out all kinds of personal insurance policies against this happening. It'll-never-happen attitudes are understandable when one grows up in an atmosphere of local defeatism, which in turn encourages a fear of everybody uniting around a common purpose.

According to sociological researchers such as Basil Bernstein, etc., working-class kids have not learnt skills to deal with the language-communication problems that organized meetings present. However, the real question for socialist youth organizers to answer is: Is there an organizational *structure* that *can* be communicated and has a basis in the spontaneity of the kids?

Organizing these meetings may have posed problems, but it was clear that the demands of the kids on the potential of the place, not to mention the ideas of the Youth Group, were going far beyond the mere provision of the junior and senior discos. Symptomatic were the persistent break-ins to the building, which no longer had any caretakers. People slept the night there, mucked about and had parties. Two close friends, fifteen-year-olds, actually converted one of the upstairs rooms into a sophisticated den. A cocktail bar – marked as such! – a faded three-piece suite, a record-player. The place may have been a bit cold but they had a glowing hearth depicted in brilliant colours on the wall. Frank and Terry's den was their unprompted attempt to renovate the dark and dusty upstairs and make it fit for habitation, a place where they could have parties, act out their fantasies, enjoy a little domestic autonomy.

One could say that a demand was being expressed in various, sometimes open, sometimes more devious ways, for the Black Horse to become a neighbourhood youth house.

Although the most persistent cry was for more disco nights, it was outside of the disco that a group sense began to emerge. The idea of a youth paper caught on among some. A visit to the new local sports centre, a controversial place in the geopolitics of youth (see page 129), was arranged, interviews made, notes taken for the purpose of doing a feature in the paper. A core group prepared to work on the production of the paper began to emerge.

Against this background of rising expectations among the youth, there was a rising clamour among the adults to close the Black Horse down. Complaints about noise, late nights, and disturbances, and rumours of drugs, sex and other unlawful goings-on, were commonplace. Because of its location, sticking out like a sore thumb amidst the main residential blocks, all comings and goings in the Black Horse could be carefully monitored. Eyes trapped behind lace curtains, hungry for incident, worked round the clock to provide the feedback for the next day's rumours. How would the Tenants Association Committee respond to the avalanche of complaints?

The Tenants Association Committee responded in a typically contradictory way. They disclaimed responsibility for the rumoured excesses of the disco while lending credence to the rumours themselves, put the responsibility firmly on the shoulders of the Youth Group and yet made gestures towards asserting greater control themselves. Even a letter from the Chief Constable congratulating the Tenants Association on opening the disco, and pointing out that juvenile crime had dropped significantly since it opened, cut little ice.

The Youth Group pointed out that the rumours were unfounded, that there had been little or no bother, that the Committee knew that, and that the real solution was to develop activities for other age groups so that all sections would have an equal stake in the Black Horse and their Tenants Association.

Even if they had wanted to do any of these things, the Tenants Association Committee was far too immobile by the spring of 1974, scarcely able to guarantee its own survival. There were serious rifts within the Committee itself. There was a power struggle for the vacant chairmanship. There were deepening rivalries with the Open Space Committee, who stirred up the discontent of the tenants against their Tenants Association. There

The Fall of the Black Horse Disco

was the reluctance of the GLC to commit themselves finally to providing the finance to rehabilitate the Black Horse. And there was the patent failure of the Tenants Association to put any real pressure on them.

Alarmed by the deteriorating situation, Community Organizer Gerry Stern advised the Tenants Association to call a public meeting, officially to re-elect the committee, and then to strengthen its rank and file support through a system of block representatives. Extensive leafleting. The night of the meeting cold and wet. Only four tenants turned up, and one belligerent member of the rival Open Space Committee. The Youth Group, other interested community workers, the Tenants Committee itself, plus some twenty members of the disco made up the gathering. The kids, who had been alerted that the disco was under threat, had come once again to stake their claim, and to demand an extension of activities. They kept good order throughout – that they had shown enough interest to attend a Tenants Association meeting was remarkable enough in itself. (Apart from which, they constituted (potentially) the largest block vote.)

Opening the meeting the chairman sized up the situation at a glance. He literally discounted the kids, and informed the meeting that there were only four people present.

The course of the meeting was to create a point of no return for the struggle to build the Black Horse as a viable community centre. To begin with, the very constitutionality of the meeting, and of the Committee itself, was challenged by the Open Space Committee faction. Points of order flashed from floor to platform. It was left to the kids to make explicit the realpolitik of the situation. Who rules the estate? Which firm? Us or Them? 'He's not really interested in this place, he's just come here to make trouble. He thinks he's the big boss round here!' (This to the vast embarrassment of the adults, of course.)

As the meeting dragged on, the kids' impatience grew. They wanted to talk about the disco *now*. However, the chairman insisted on treating this as item 6 on the agenda, any other business, and his youthful audience as none of his business. The kids left in disgust. In failing to recognize the importance of their youth constituency, and its demands for representation, the Tenants Association had begun to dig its own grave.

After this, things began to go rapidly downhill. The Youth Group were increasingly isolated from the tenants. The kids were without a voice. The pub had been evacuated by its care-takers. Resources began to fail, and the Council were reluctant to intervene financially. Finally the Black Horse was abandoned to the mercy of a divided and rancorous community.

The Youth Group made a last-ditch attempt to save the situation. A benefit concert was arranged with a top-name group, and publicized in the local and underground press. The disco was repainted and carpeted. On the big night, reinforcements arrived in the shape of large numbers of rock afficionados who took over the saloon bar of the Cross Keys while they were waiting for the band – much to the disgust of the local villain clientele: 'Bleeding hippies – whatever next?' For the first time, a section of the older youth of the area paid a visit – a hard crew mostly in their early twenties. They had got a sniff that something was up.

There was definitely a sense of occasion, but underneath trouble was brewing. The regulars enjoyed the concert, but rightly re-sented the hippy invasion. Towards the end of the evening, a number of fights broke out. The local scrap-men, who had been patiently waiting for just such a denouement, assessed that this was the time to strike. A number of them were found in the basement attempting to hoist certain valuable items through the trap-door. Archie Jones tried to remonstrate with them and got an iron bar in his face for his trouble. Archie had been one of the most progressive and hard workers of the tenants – his attempt to organize his community had brought him three days in hospital.

In April 1974, fire swept through the basement and ground floor of the Black Horse disco. It had been started deliberately, in the basement. A gas pipe had even been severed to precipitate an explosion. A few days before, the whole building had been systematically and efficiently wrecked. Toilet bowls had been shattered, electrical wirings uprooted, doors ripped off their hinges, panels torn out of the bar and stage. Everything from light switches to radiators and gas fittings had been carefully put out of commission.

The wrecking of the Black Horse and the subsequent fire – to finish the job – was quite unlike the careless damage the place had occasionally suffered at the hands of the kids. When the place was broken into by the kids after the caretakers had moved out, it was remarkable how little damage was done, considering the high spirits that would prevail. Carelessly tossed beer cans, fire extinguishers let off, graffiti painted on the walls. But as the example of Frank and Terry's room shows, the kids had their own code for their private use of the place, which all except the loners like Kelly tended to obey.

The wrecking and then firing of the disco was quite clearly the work of hands other than the kids'. It was a professional job. Three men had been seen entering the place – with a key – shortly before the wrecking was discovered. They, if it was they, had worked quietly, professionally, unemotionally. Who were they? One is tempted to say simply the self-appointed executioners of the sentence of this community on the 'notorious' old pub that had become a community centre, which had become a disco, which was rapidly turning into a youth house.

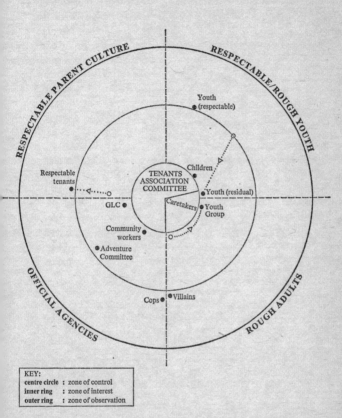

Black Horse: Junior and senior disco (November 1973).

Part Two
Configurations of Youth

Territoriality

By now the reader may well feel that all the rituals of 'territoriality' on the Monmouth, with its nasty overtones of violence,
simply boil down to a 'biological instinct' and are some kind of
throwback to a more primitive – or even animal – society. After
all, the argument goes, if you force people to live in an overcrowded concrete jungle, you must expect them to behave occasionally like a somewhat less evolved species of primate! Unfortunately the evidence is that human territoriality is a *symbolic*
process, whose complexities go well beyond the capabilities of
even the most intelligent and social of animal species, even to the
point of escaping the comprehension of the most intelligent and
social-minded of the human beings who study them, and who
persist in arguing by analogies from one set of data to the
other.

What we refer to as 'territoriality' is a symbolic process of
magically appropriating, owning and controlling the material
environment in which you live, but which in real, economic and
political terms is owned and controlled by 'outsiders' – in our
society, by private landlords or the State. It applies, therefore,
almost exclusively to working-class areas. And it has to be understood in class terms.

In Britain, the defeat of the political culture which culminated
in the Chartist movement produced as its legacy community
structures which evolved inwardly, and served to create an almost
separate society. The sense of place, of neighbourhood, became
intimately bound up with a sense of class, a sense of one's place
in society. And, since the 1840s, this fact has been exploited by
town-planners and municipal reformers, who, for very different
reasons, saw the political advantages of having a parochialized

working class, split up into small units, each divided against the other by fierce local loyalties.*

Territoriality is, therefore, deeply ingrained in most working-class parent cultures, even if its functions are diffused through a number of institutions: the local pub and shops, and local political, religious, and cultural associations of every kind. But the kids have only one institution to support this function, and a fragile one at that – the 'gang'. The same historical processes which pushed the parent culture inwards on itself pushed working-class youth to its periphery, as the residual legatees of street culture.

So the street becomes the arena where the Growing Up Game is played, a social space and time of apparent freedom from the more insidious forms of parental censorship and control. Here the peer group assembles itself, to enact its rivalries, and so the game of identities and differences between the sexes and between the generations can begin.† In early childhood this takes the form of fantasy games; later, without losing this component, it takes on a more organized ritual form, and finally becomes elaborated by teenagers into collective narratives or myth, at a time when the game is getting rather more serious. The basic rule of this game is not that 'any numbers can play', but rather that certain people can't. Because they are too little or too big. Because they are boys or girls. So at the heart of the Game lies a symbolic interdict, but one which in this particular environment has no material support.‡ Any numbers *could* play: the bomb site and

---

* Today populists of the extreme Right and extreme Left, obviously for vastly different motives, continue this tradition, urging the preservation of or return to the close-knit 'urban village' as the bulwark of the people's liberties, against the power of the centralized bureaucracies at Westminster, and more recently Brussels.

† The Law which determines the parameters of this game could be formulated like this – sexual identity: generational difference: sexual difference: generational identity. This law is usually called after the hero of an ancient Greek myth – Oedipus.

‡ We do not mean the highly structured gang, organised into different age grades, each with its own hierarchy, etc. These occur only if there are strong ethnic and/or territorial rivalries between interfacing parent cultures, as in Catholic–Protestant interzones in Liverpool, Glasgow, or Belfast. The

street are there for all. This opens up a whole possible area of ambiguity, of distance and relation between the sexes and generations. The function of territoriality is quite simply to eliminate this problem at its source, by providing a material basis for a system of *positional* rules which preserve the boundaries of the loose-knit peer-group network in the street, and assign the entire youthful population – big and little, boy and girl – to a place which cuts across these distinctions, a place which is marked by an unequivocal question: Friend or Foe.

As we shall see, the question is posed in a way which already contains its own answer in an inverted form, irrespective of whether the affinity–enmity conflict involves traditions of feud between groups, or isolated incidents between individuals who may not even know each other. Territoriality is never not a *social* process. You may feel that you belong on the Packington estate, just like your mum and dad do. But you will never belong in the Packington – one of the Arsenal North Bank's top fighting crews – until you demonstrate that symbolically the area belongs to you. And that demands a ritual display of aggravation against a rival crew. The logic of this whole process therefore comes out best in accounts of fights. Here is one such account:

Whenever you have parties, there's one thing you should never do, is invite kids from two different areas like – say – round here and the Angel . . . never invite kids like that, 'cos they're so close, yet they're so far apart, if you see what I mean. I went to this party, that was a liberty. There was this fight, see, it was over this bird, Sharon, and my mate Rusty starts having a go at her. He says to her 'Bird, or no bird, you need a slap,' Whack! She starts screaming at him: 'You wait, I'll get my bloke.' So he says: 'Go and get him.' So her bloke comes back and says to Rusty, 'Did you hit my bird?' 'Yeah.' So he says, 'All right then, outside.' And he starts giving him a kicking and so I was fighting his younger brother. But Sharon's sister's gone and got her brother's mates and they jump in on me and so Rusty's bird's brother jumps in . . . There was a bit of a ruck, and there were three other kids with the bloke who was having a go at Rusty, and one of them threw a

---

interdict here become explicitly parental: because they are Proddies, etc. And very material.

bottle at the ceiling and it smashed everywhere. But that fight was broke up and I went outside, and there was this bloke from the party and he started saying, 'A kid in a white shirt threw it' and I had a white shirt on, and he said it again, and he was looking at me, 'a kid in a white shirt'. So I said to him, 'Look,' I said, 'it weren't me,' but he kept on saying it and the way he was looking at me. I said to him, 'Go away, will yer.' And I turned me back and walked back into the party and he sort of whacked me. I fell on the floor, I was kickin' me feet up in his face, he couldn't get near me. Then someone pulled him off . . . It was silly really. You could say there were three lots: there was us, there was the kids from the Angel, and these kids who'd come with this bird, Sharon. The kids from the Angel, they know some of us, and we know some of them, and one of our lot, Johnny, was fighting one of the other lot Sharon was with, but when the Angel seen it, they thought Johnny wasn't with us like, he was with the other lot, 'cos they didn't know him, of course, and they thought he was starting all the trouble, so they're all running to hit him, and we were running into them to help him. And like, it's almost like us fighting the Angel, 'cos of these other four kids with Sharon who weren't with anyone, if you know what I mean. They was brought there to stop trouble and they started it. That was the only thing that was wrong . . . they invited kids from different areas, which is all wrong . . .

The complexities of this account have nothing to do with any failure by the speaker to conceptualize what is going on. The restrictions of its syntax are those of narrative structure as such. The speaker is explaining a complex system of rules, concretely, through the description of an event in which they were violated, and we challenge the reader to produce a better, more logically connected account. In fact, the whole thing could be read as a kind of talmudic commentary, whose intricacies could only be rendered more economically by being translated into a meta-language, such as the abstract propositions of symbolic logic. The territorial rule which is being broken is clearly stated:

That was the only thing that was wrong . . . they invited kids from different areas, which is all wrong . . .

But underneath this lies a system of relations defining affinity and enmity, who's on whose side, in what situation, here very much stated in the context of kinship and its obligations. These rules could be put formally as a set of propositions:

1. The friend of a friend is a friend.
$$+ \quad\quad + \quad = \quad +$$

2. The enemy of an enemy is a friend.
$$- \quad\quad - \quad = \quad +$$

3. The friend of an enemy is an enemy.
$$+ \quad\quad - \quad = \quad -$$

4. The enemy of a friend is an enemy.
$$- \quad\quad + \quad = \quad -$$

These propositions can be built up on each other to the nth degree, without destroying the symmetry of the rule; for example, the friend of an enemy's enemy's friend is still a friend.

The system serves to support and structure the interlocking social networks which expand outwards from the family, through the peer group to the solidarities of school and workplace. But this also contains a problem. Friend and enemy are categories which define each other by exclusion. But as the rule expands through a network, it may generate feedback loops in which 'John' finds himself simultaneously assigned to opposite categories by others in the group who, nevertheless, are applying the rule consistently throughout. But where rules are positional – here, quite literally, a function of place – no one can be friend *and* enemy without dissolving the whole system into an infinitely negotiable see-saw of person-to-person perceptions. When this happens, 'John' is caught in an untenable position in the network, the inevitable focus and scapegoat of its tensions. This would be a chronic occurrence if the only categories in play were friend and enemy. But each logically implies a negative 'qualifier' – 'not a friend', 'not an enemy' – and these are less strongly marked oppositions, and give the system the necessary flexibility to integrate people like 'John' by assigning them to a relative position between the two extremes of affinity or enmity. The way these four sets interact could be mapped as follows:

These are the means which enable people to locate each other, confidently and with precision, on a scale between best mates and worst enemies. Fortunately, in the real world they don't require the assistance of logicians to do this!

These operations are not derived from abstract ideas about friendship and so on, but are a system of ideological practices which are all too painfully concrete: the rituals of recognition which regulate everyday encounters, all the way from the simplest of routine greetings to the most elaborate ceremonial challenge. In working-class cultures, recognition is always of a *difference*, either one that is shared and therefore releases a display of friendliness, or one that isn't, which releases a show of hostility. If such rituals also involve a *mis*recognition it is because these differences are interpreted as contingent 'qualities' emanating from – and hidden – 'inside' the individuals, rather than what they are: the structural properties of a system of relationships governed by positional rules. It is a misrecognition of the grounds of *identity*.

Frequently, individuals enter the social field of the peer group whose positions are not contextually, that is territorially, defined. They are simultaneously 'not a friend' and 'not an enemy'. The group's strategy therefore consists in attempting to provoke the 'stranger' into the public declaration of a difference which will enable him to be located as One of Us (friend) or One of Them (enemy). For working-class kids the paradigm of recognition takes the form of ritual insult.

At its simplest not a word is spoken. Just a silent exchange of glances: taking a screw at someone – someone taking a screw at you.* This may be only the first stage of an escalating sequence which culminates in a punch-up. In between a whole repertoire

* At the level of fantasy, *and only there*, this kind of 'screwing' has the same connotation as the other kinds (i.e. sexual and criminal): breaking in to a forbidden 'inside' belonging to somebody else.

of insult may be displayed, which includes repartee, taking the piss, practical jokes, and so on. This is the base-line of a whole working-class tradition of wit and humour, which provides the material for the stand-up comic of music hall and working-men's club, just as it sensitizes the kids to the linguistic and other skills involved.

Now imagine the situation of a young middle-class teacher or youth worker with a progressive outlook, confronting a group of working-class kids. Culturally, it is an encounter between strangers, and each side brings its own rules into play to deal with the situation. The teacher will be motivated to establish non-authoritarian relationships with the kids – to be defined as their friend. And he goes about befriending them, using the techniques he has learnt for establishing relationships with strangers in his own social milieu. He will try to *negotiate* an area of common *subjectivity*, based on eliciting signs of *similarity*, in this instance perhaps by trying to create contexts which will demonstrate elective affinities in terms of a generational life-style, for example rock 'n' roll, movies, clothes, and so on. The kids, however, will be mobilizing their resources to elicit from him expressions of difference as a function of his objective position – and may be making jokes about his appearance, mannerisms, accent, and so on. The teacher has two options. He can turn the other cheek to the kids cheeking him. In which case, they will probably consign him to a residual category – not a friend, not an enemy, but a mug – and the insults will simply escalate. Or else he can stand on his dignity, lose his temper and assert his authority by threats or actual punishment. In this case, the kids have won anyway, because they have located him unambiguously as an enemy.

The problem for the teacher then is to decide at what level to respond. Is the kids' behaviour good-humoured 'play', in which case he can just play along with it? Or is it real aggression, calling for counter-measures? There is no way for him to step outside the communication frame so as to tell. And whichever way he responds, he is unlikely to be vindicated by the kids' responses. If he plays along, then he has lost control, and the kids may not stop short of trying to wreck the classroom or youth club. But if he cracks down, the kids may turn round and accuse him of misreading the situation – he can't take a joke, and so on – and he's lost the one thing he was trying to achieve, a friendly, easygoing relationship with them.

The distinction between this use of ritual insult and the techniques of the wind-up merchant is one of degree rather than kind. The latter is simply more professional in his approach to his victim, more conscious of the mechanism he is manipulating. Both play on a special effect created by articulating two different kinds of statements:

1. Those that are simply *informative* about a state of affairs, in which the speaker is not necessarily represented as the grammatical subject, and where the utterance itself does not affect the social context in which it is made. As opposed to

2. *performative* statements, in which the speaker is always present as the grammatical subject; through the process of utterance, he enacts the reality his statement denotes, and/or defines the social context in which it takes place.

For example: A youth is up at a magistrates' court on a charge. He is asked if he pleads guilty or not guilty. If he pleads guilty, then that is defined as a performative statement; he is judged to have judged himself. If he pleads not guilty, however, this is treated as purely informative. He is then called on to the witness stand to take an oath to tell the truth. This is technically a performative statement, but since he is the defendant, and since we are talking about a bourgeois legal process, this carries little weight. He is then cross-examined, all his statements being treated as purely informative. When it is the police's turn to take the same oath, its performative resonance is read as carrying right through their evidence. The magistrates then give their verdict and pass sentence (performative statements). In our society the ability to make performative statements is the virtual monopoly of the class whose job it is to lay down the law, open garden fetes, close factories, and launch ships or party political manifestos. It is power which legitimates these kinds of statements, just as they in turn legitimate these people's authority.

But there is a special case where those with no power and no authority make use of performative statements as a means to exert control over each other, or against those in authority over them. And that case is ritual insult. For example:

One evening on the Wall by Monmouth estate, Tommy arrives looking like David Bowie, complete with make-up and streaked hair. Chorus of hoots, wolf whistles, and jeers from the Wall gang. Then Mick, who used to be a close friend of Tommy's but is now more involved with his motor bike, starts to have a go at him. 'Where's your handbag, dearie? Going out with your fella, then? You little fairy.' Ruffles Tommy's hair. Tommy is trapped. On the face of it, he is confronted with a simple informative statement: You're a fairy, which he could deny on the same level: No, I'm not. But Mick's insult contains a meta-statement which pre-empts this response; an injunction which says: Go on then, if you're not a fairy, then show us you're not. The obvious way for Tommy to show the Wall gang that he is not in fact weak, effeminate, passive, or in any other way like a fairy as far as they are concerned is to smash Mick in the face. But Mick is bigger, and a better fighter. Tommy would lose and be humiliated in the process – showing himself to be weak. And Mick knows all this as well as Tommy and so do the other members of the Wall gang. The only other option open to Tommy is to cap Mick's insult with a counter-gibe which is equally effective. But he's not much good at repartee – certainly not up to Mick's standard. So he just stands there for a moment, red-faced, and then drifts off, promising revenge under his breath. His departure is followed by more jeers and whistles. What has happened is that Mick's original statement has assumed a real performative function. Tommy has *become* in his own eyes, and in those of his mates, even if temporarily, a 'fairy'.

Here is another example where the mechanism is even clearer. A boy and a girl are playing together. The boy is four, the girl five.

BOY (*chanting*): You're a baby, you're a baby.
GIRL (*crossly*): No, I'm not. I'm five. I'm older than you. And bigger than you, so there.

BOY: No, you're not. You're a baby. Yes you are, you're a baby.
GIRL (*now very upset*): I'm *not* a baby. I'm not. I'm NOT.
BOY: Yes you are, etc.
At which point the girl bursts into tears and runs away calling for her mum.
BOY (*triumphantly calling after her*): See, I told you, you *are* a baby.

Ritual insults are mostly likely to lead to physical injury, when there is no way of walking, as opposed to talking, your way out. But then what counts is not a reputation for wit, but for hardness, for being able to handle yourself in a fight.

As the terms suggest these are techniques of bodily control which put the practice of motor skills (climbing, running, etc.) at the disposal of mastering the immediate environment of the working-class city. Being able to settle disputes with your fists, also ensures that your words need no further emphasis!

Techniques of cognitive and bodily control, not only serve the same social function, in establishing distance and closure, the boundaries between Us and Them, they also derive from a common symbolic order, to which the working-class child has traditionally been apprenticed. This order can perhaps be most easily observed, where both techniques are most strenuously practised, and locked together – street games.

These games have usually been classified according to differences in their surface features; different types of activities (seeking, chasing, duelling ...) or different local or regional characteristics (dialect, historical colourations). But perhaps these could be most usefully regarded as so many empirical variations of an underlying structure, at once formal and elementary. We suggest that the work this unconscious structure does, through the practices it sustains, is to link the dialectics of identity and difference to those of separation and possession.

One of the most popular chasing games played around the Monmouth, by both sexes, and assorted age groups from seven to fourteen, was called Cops and Robbers. Two teams are chosen, this in itself being an important element of foreplay, as preferences and animosities are sorted out. Then a base is decided on and marked out. The scenario is that the robbers have pulled a bank job, and the cops have to arrest them before they can get back to the safety of 'home'. The game ends when all the robbers either have been caught or have made base, the teams then swopping roles, the winning team being whichever has the most homes after an agreed series of games.

At first sight it seems a simple enough chasing game; but it's not enough for the robbers to simply evade the clutches of the Law, they have to get to base to do so; equally the cops not only have to get their man, but usually to do so *beyond* a certain agreed distance from base. It's not enough for one team to simply defend the base, or the other to get as far away from them as possible; the rules of the game prohibit such a stalemate. Much of the tactical skill, and enjoyment, consists in the way both sides try to outmanoeuvre each other, the robbers perhaps using a decoy to draw the copy away, the cops in turn attempting to lure them into a trap through taunts and gibes.

These rules derive from a system of formal oppositions. They bear initially on an instance of separation or lack (of the robbers from home, of cops from robber) which assigns a task, whose successful accomplishment demands the overcoming of certain obstacles by means of a variety of ruses; success in turn produces an instance of possession ('safety' or 'arrest') which supresses the original lack. Like all systems of competitive rules, the game pivots on an interdict, whose violation signifies failure. The system could be represented as follows:

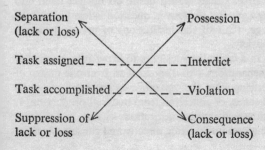

Separation (lack or loss)	Possession
Task assigned	Interdict
Task accomplished	Violation
Suppression of lack or loss	Consequence (lack or loss)

Configurations of Youth

In the case of 'Cops and Robbers':

	SEPARATION	INTERDICT	VIOLATION	POSSESSION
ROBBER	to get back home	without being caught by cops	is caught	gets to safety
COP	to catch robber	before the robber gets home	fails to make arrest	catches robber
	task assigned		failure	success

It is no coincidence that what is found embedded in these games, is the same system of symbolic functions which as object relations (of identity and difference), rule the subject's means of being his or her age and sex. What is being occupied in the game is nothing but a series of places of desire, of exchanges between them marked by the presence or absence of their object. Yet instead of being locked inside the family, and its fantasy systems of theft and gift, debt and sacrifice, instead of being frozen in an untenable or overtenanted place in the parental discourse, these games, and the whole material culture of working-class childhood, enable people to 'play' with all these places, and in a supportive social setting outside adult censorship. The same historical forces which confined the political aspirations of the class to the limits of occupation or community, also produced a system of extra-familial apprenticeship which was a profoundly anti-oedipal device. This does not imply that kids do not use these settings and structures perversely, i.e. individually, as means of 'getting their own back' for losses or lacks inflicted by 'other scenes'; nor that these street games named desire do not get them into trouble with the Law. But the Law in question is less likely to be that of language, than of the institutions of private property and public propriety.

Growing up in a capitalist society is to grow into a series of quite *material* separations – of dispossession from the means of production, deriving from the separation of the family from its means of subsistence, of education from material production. It is these separations, which those institutions legalize, and guarantee. Yet no one grows up by living directly and consciously these separations, but through their inversion into imaginary contexts of belonging or appropriation, which in the case of working-class culture also challenges the ideological premises of property and propriety.

However to become grown up is also to have grown out of these 'kids games' and to discover new and more material ways of being your age and sex. Increasingly it also means to be confined to a special space of social isolation; for in the advanced capitalist city there are few legitimate places for working-class youth to be, which remain outside the control of propriety – even the depopulated streets are officially 'out of bounds'.

Having nothing to do, having nowhere to go, equals boredom. Working-class kids are already apprenticed to the condition at school, in preparation for their working lives. Yet they escape from the tedium of classroom or workshop into 'free time' only to encounter there another variant of the same; in dealing with it, they bring to bear not just the techniques they have learnt to interrupt oppressive routines elsewhere, but those they have mastered earlier in dealing with the immediate environment of childhood. 'Mucking about' takes on an added dimension when it gets to grips with the specific boredom of free time – a lack of *being* as much as having, or doing. Above all a lack of consequence.

Killing boredom means making something happen out of nothing. An action that produces a consequence, becomes an event; an event is whatever is remarkable, recountable to your mates. 'Mucking about' thus becomes subsumed under rules and rituals which gives it narrative functions; and these in turn correspond to the same symbolic order which regulates street games. The tasks the peer group assigns itself to suppress its lack of being always and already bear on specific interdicts – the do's and don'ts which rule their lives. In this game of consequences, it is never just a question of having – or doing – this or that; it is the way the group possesses itself, a means of coming alive; to infringe an interdict successfully yields up stories spiced with obstacles overcome, ruses worked; failure equals the ignominious return to boredom and inconsequence.

The following account is of one episode in a continuous and

collective narrative given to us by a sixteen-year-old lad from the Denby estate:

> Well, one night, we was just walking about, not doing nothing, you know, and then Billy says 'Let's go up the market,' and then Jacko sees this ladder and he starts mucking about on it, and we get up on it, on to the roof of this shop, and its a flat roof and there's all this gear lying about, old chairs, telly the lot, and Jacko says we could get a few bob for scrap. And then Billy, he's looking out for us, and he starts screaming, 'Here comes the Old Bill,' so we scarper quick don't we . . . but they wasn't really, he was having us on, so we weren't too pleased I can tell you, but it was all a load of rubbish there really, so we went home.

This particular story relies for its dramatic effect on the ambiguities of what is playful and what is serious; what begins as killing boredom by larking about on a ladder, shifts into a proposition to make money by contravening certain sections of the Theft Act. Billy however gets bored, and so creates an event on his own account. By crying wolf for the Law, he not only interrupts the serious business, but exposes the element of pretend in the whole *mise en scène*. His mates are angry, but perhaps also secretly relieved; Billy's wind-up at least forestalled any serious consequence, while still conforming to the rules of this game: he knew his mates had no means of knowing whether the alarm was real or not, in this context the ruse constitutes a performative statement. They let him off, because he has done the same for them. In symbolic terms the task they set themselves has been successfully accomplished, any dissonances of pride in daring taken care of by the sour grapes effect, it was not worth the trouble nicking anyway, and so they go home, everyone's honour satisfied.

In looking round for materials to fabricate remarkable events with, kids tend to seize on whatever is nearest at hand. That means violating a territorial interdict which has done more than anything to introduce the ideologies of private property and public propriety into working-class cultures: don't shit on your own doorstep (if you want to draw the line under your own feet). This interdict not only demarcates between rough and respectable, but reproduces its terms on either side of the great moral divide, in a series of infinite gradations of social status. Killing boredom, though, is not done by attacking ideologies as such, but by attacking the physical plant in which political economy has enshrined them. Here theft and destruction are equivalent, and equally accessible modes of action. On the Monmouth, smashing windows, setting fire to derelict houses, damaging cars, were junior versions of older brothers exploits in breaking and entering, or take-and-drive-aways.

Since the first construction of mass estates, vandalism has been the number one problem for tenants organizations and housing authorities alike. Repairs on some estates can more than double the annual maintenance costs, and become a major item of deficit in public-housing finance. A whole gamut of solutions have been proposed – more police surveillance, local vigilante patrols, mobile trouble-shooters, the reintroduction of resident caretakers, adventure playgrounds, youth clubs. But whether these proposals aim at prevention or cure, repression or safety-valves, they are united in lumping together quite disparate behaviours under the common denominator, and more importantly, seeing in them only material, not discursive, practices.

Yet what goes under the name of vandalism should perhaps be seen as an attempt to reassert rules of territoriality, *foci* and boundaries of peer-group rivalries, in a social space which has become virtually illegible for this purpose, and not least through the intervention of town-planners. In some inner-city neighbourhoods, the only way for the youth to assert the dialectics of belonging, is to efface, or deface, the official landscape, in favour of landmarks of their own which they create in so doing. However indefensible such behaviour may appear, it is the only means at their disposal to build a defensible space.

Ironically, the more enlightened attempts to deal with the problem by providing local youth with places to be, and things to do, only end by opening up new arenas for vandalism. Such leisure activities may be authorized, but by the same token, the kids themselves are not the authors. So, far from killing boredom, they call for the creation of remarkable events.

The reason for this is not hard to find. The byzantine processes whereby local government provides such facilities are almost completely invisible, or incomprehensible, to their users. It is something They do for Us. But if these facilities are given, kids over about eleven are well aware that they have not been made a present of them. These places do not in fact belong to them either in the sense of economic ownership, or political control. Yet the organizers want *members*, active adherents to some normative ideal, not just passive consumers. So they tend to construct imaginary settings of belonging. Painting the Youth Club. The Members committee. Secondly these facilities operate with formal rules of territorial inclusion (the catchment area) and informal rules of ideological exclusion (public propriety). The result then is twofold. The provision tends to detonate existing patterns of territorial affinity and enmity, as rival groups struggle to assert magical forms of ownership or control. Secondly they trigger behaviour designed to test empirically whether in fact these facilities do belong to the youth, are theirs to do what they like with. In either case, waves of petty theft and vandalism ensue, and as long as this continues, these places serve to kill boredom, if not in quite the way intended.

The positions taken up within the youth constituency towards such provision, whether as active members, users, or actors at a distance, serve to reiterate the rough/respectable distinctions within the parent culture. But no longer in any simple or direct way.

The divisions of labour at the point of production, between skilled and unskilled, are not only themselves being eroded, but are no longer reproduced in the moral economy of the working-class neighbourhood. The old labour aristocracy (in our area of print and railway workers) may have once succeeded in living apart in micro-districts of their own, just as they succeeded in spinning a cocoon of institutions – mechanics institutes, clubs, friendly societies, which made substantive, if not absolute, the connection between superior occupational and moral status. Equally, casual and unskilled labour may have elaborated more rudimentary forms of social closure – in their oral and fighting traditions. But these systems of cultural apprenticeship have largely broken down, as has the great divide between them. In the mass estates of the inner city black and white, skilled and unskilled, established and outsiders, self-employed and unemployed, hard men and soft touches, live together in no pre-established terms of harmony or conflict. The sense of place and of class are no longer so intimately tied together. Other means have to be found to re-establish the broken links in the chains of cultural transmission. And through these means, too, the division of labour, rather than the unity of the class, is enlarged.

Knuckle Sandwich

Forms of 'hardness' can still be anchored in street-fighting traditions where these survive; the Monmouth and Denby estates, with their complement of second- and third-generation Irish families, still contained the traces. Accounts of Famous Fights were passed from father to son in local families. Phil would rhapsodize at length to his mates about the time old man MacIlroy, half-pissed, had taken on all the menfolk of his very extended family at a sister's wedding, and still had time to call for more beer. Young Neil told how old man Allen had one day for a bet drawn a line across the bar-room floor at the Black Horse, and challenged all comers to cross it; he won his bet. These legends are not just part of a rich oral tradition; they are also supposed to instruct the next generation, how, where and when to put their boots and fists, and the occasional broken bottle, where their mouths are.

In faithfully recounting these stories, Phil and Neil were carrying on a discourse which speaks to a shrinking audience. In earlier years much family talk would have been sustained by a whole network of popular institutions which linked into a wider community context, and even into the professional fight game. It is no coincidence that professional fighters have traditionally been recruited from the ranks of first-generation immigrant families struggling to survive in a hostile environment. Irish, Jews, Blacks – all have successively thrown up champions. Rinty Monahan, Kid Berg, Harry Mizler, Bunny Sterling: these are the names remembered in the annals of the British fight game. But at street level, there were thousands of lads from similar backgrounds who sought to emulate them.

Before the war a young man would first show promise with his fists in neighbourhood gangs. These fights were not just to defend territory but to assert the physical integrity of the parent culture, which was under attack in so many other ways. The next step might have been for friends, or workmates, to put up money to arrange a fight 'on the stones', perhaps to decide who was neighbourhood champion. Sometimes fights were arranged between champions of rival ethnic groups or different areas.

Fights on the stones had their own rules – though not exactly the Marquess of Queensberry's. In the factory yard or the back alley, a crowd of interested parties would gather, most of whom had bets on the outcome. Friends would officiate in the corners, and you were judged to have lost when you could no longer carry on. Many contests would be catchweight – a small wiry man fighting a larger would provide an added David and Goliath fascination. Throughout the proceedings, a trusted member of the fraternity would 'hold the purse' (the bets laid) for all to see, while another would keep a lookout for the police.

These fights were not only an important apprenticeship into the fight game itself. A good street fighter would attract the attention of the network of local patrons of boxing. These were usually self-made men – the timber merchant, the publican, the haulage contractor, and other variety of the species – the local fixers, bookies, fences, 'scrap dealers', the villains, many of them ex-fighters themselves. Patronage could take various forms. In the field of heavy casual labour, where work could be an extension of training (most notably in the markets and docks), 'a word in your ear' would get the young novice preferential treatment. If a lad showed he was coming good in his early fights, patrons would readily be found to put up money for promotions, where money could be made. Not by the lad, of course. Most of his earnings would be taken by the manager, trainer and so on. All these were needed before the boxer could obtain a licence and be allowed to fight. Most professional fighters remained part-time. The young novice's earnings from the ring was simply a supplementary income, from a few shillings for taking on all comers at the fairground booth to a few pounds for a night's work at Shoreditch Town Hall. But even this was useful when times were hard, as they so often were during this period, especially for immigrant families.

Graduation into the ranks of the professionals inevitably excluded the novice from the street-fighting scene or the bar-room brawl. To get involved outside the ring would mean losing his licence, and a severer than usual sentence from the magistrates. Nevertheless, the status as well as the stigma of his early background followed him into the ring. A two-fisted style of fighting evoked echoes of street culture and its underlife, and this was recognized by an audience composed equally of his local following and 'the experts'. A fighter like Pat Rafferty or 'Two Ton Tony' Galento, good at settling arguments with their bare fists but found out in the ring, constitute a central legend of professional boxing. The fighter against the boxer, brawn against brains, instinct against science – such archetypal oppositions are contested in flesh and blood and give the boxing spectacle much of its conscious drama.

Into this exclusively working-class domain, the boys' club movement at the turn of the century attempted to introduce a different ethos. The amateur code of the gentleman stressed the virtues of fitness, consistent training, abstention from vices such as drinking and smoking, and above all the art of being a good loser, rather than a born one. The club gymnasium rather than the back alley was the place to learn to box properly, yet it was still a manly place for boys to settle arguments. By the 1920s, in London clubs like the Gainsford Covent Garden and Repton in the East End, boxing was disinfected of its unsavoury connections with gambling and petty crime, not without some tension of course between the small hall boys and the grafters, and the advocates of self-improvement through self-defence, as each competed to recruit youngsters to their respective codes.

Today, with the obvious exception of the black immigrant community, recruitment into boxing, both professional and amateur, is confined to a diminishing number of old-established 'fighting families' (for example the Walkers of the East End, the Mancinis of Notting Hill, the Straceys of Bethnal Green, the Tibbs of South London gang fame). The fight game itself has become a backwater of remembrance of an ageing fraternity, while the amateur tradition of the boys' club has been left behind in the slipstream of post-war youth culture. The distance between the rituals of the ring and those of contemporary teenage violence has assumed the proportions of a great divide; while the first have ossified into an almost perversely formal ceremonial, the latter have become increasingly unstructured.

Sixteen-year-old Bobby Munro was generally recognized as the best fighter for his age on the Monmouth; so good in fact that he complained that no one would take him on. He enjoyed a scrap 'as long as its fair and friendly' but he wouldn't pick a fight 'to get the practice' because it only got you into more trouble, i.e. it would be breaking the code. Why didn't he solve the problem by learning boxing at a nearby youth club, which specialized in the noble art? This advice was anathema to him. Youth club boxing and his own fighting culture were for him totally incompatible. It wasn't just that the techniques were different; they represented two different moral universes.

And he wasn't going to change sides. At school his expertise at sabotaging classroom order and his reputation with his fists had been equally recognized by a succession of teachers, who tried in vain to persuade him to develop the latter skill through boxing for the school, as a way of getting him to abandon the former! But as far as Bobby was concerned, boxing was unnatural. 'We was given fists to fight with. If we'd 've been meant to fight with them things [boxing gloves] we'd 've been born with them . . . All them geezers running around with skipping ropes, they're like a load of nances.'

Bobby came from a fighting family. Thirty years previously his father had successfully made the transition from street fighter to boxer, precisely through the youth club. Lads of that earlier generation and background could never have made a statement like Bobby's – that boxing was soft. But in the intervening period, the occupational or other close-knit community structures which had supported the father's solution have disintegrated – whether through urban redevelopment or changes in the division of labour.

Yet a more positive force finally prevented Bobby following his father's steps into the ring. The post-war period saw not just the decline of local boxing traditions, but subcultures whose styles and idioms constituted a non place realm of identity for massive sections of working-class youth (i.e. teds, mods, rockers, skinheads, greasers). This meant that for the first time fighting techniques were no longer regulated, and transmitted through the parent culture, but directly through the peer groupings of youth. Certain aspects of the old 'hardness' were conserved, but only as a purely symbolic element of ritual display, integrated along with the other systems, dress, music, argot, which in varying forms and combinations gave these subcultures their distinctive 'code'. Most recently, however, the coherence of these codes has been subsumed by traditional symbolism or else their component parts have evolved into separate, specialized and highly dissociated 'styles' or 'interests' of their own.

One product of this has been the emergence of the fighting *crew*, a legacy of the skinhead era. As the skins declined in numbers and influence, as their argot was assimilated back into the mainstream of working-class culture, as their dress was taken over by commercial interest as a generalized youth commodity, as reggae was reappropriated by black youth, or 'taken up' as a specialized 'thing', as the drugs and life-styles of middle-class youth made ideological inroads, so the elements of ritual display became increasingly impoverished, denuded of symbolic content. The one element which remained, precisely the one which had been so fetishized by the mass media as the sign of the skinhead, was 'aggro', and it was this which the rump of hard-core skinheads seized on and elaborated, in a purely material sense, as the matrix of a new style. The fighting crew was born.* Inevitably such crews developed in those areas where the subculture had been strongest and parent culture weakest. They remain locality-

* The central dynamic in the emergence of the fighting crew lies in the recent history of youth soccer culture. This is dealt with later in this section.

based, but violence is only marginally related to the protocols of territory – which now provide the pretext, rather than the structuring context of 'aggro'.

Micky Spyer was a member of one such crew in an area of South Islington which had been a skinhead stronghold.

Well, some of us go to work, and then we go to clubs, or pubs sometimes, to have fights, but the weekends are best, that's when we have the big fights, with about ten of us outside the fish and chip shop. You've got to fight to protect yourself and you can get a bit of a name and you've got to protect it, you can't just bottle it and walk away, and then you get really slagged off . . . There's about ten of us like, we're all together, all mates from round the flats . . . and when we get into fights then the birds we're with fight with the other birds [i.e. of the other crew]. They're worse than us, they use bottles as well, they're fucking mad sometimes . . . They're all good fighters in our crew, well, that's the idea, isn't it, there's a few no good, well they just hang about with us like, they're not really in it. If a kids not a good fighter than he don't go about with us and that's that. If we think a geezer's all mouth and not really a good fighter, then we just have a fight with him to show him up . . . they're the real idiots, the right mouthy geezers.'

Elements of the old fighting code can still be seen in this account, but they no longer have any work to do. The code no longer has any purchase on social reality outside itself. And not surprisingly this results in a kind of regression of age roles in the fighting crew.

The kind of routine fighting which characterizes young children's groups in the playground or street is both random and highly competitive, but still playful, essentially 'friendly'. Its function is both to learn and display fighting prowess, as well as to establish hierarchies of prestige within the peer group. The fighting crew of older youth remains fixated at this stage; the same mechanisms are carried over, but with one big difference – now they operate for 'real', and are projected on to randomly selected 'enemies' outside the group. In terms of sex roles though, this development must be seen as also containing a progressive aspect. For, as Micky's account makes clear and as our own observations corroborated, what had been a male preserve, and an index of male sexual dominance, opened up to the opposite sex. But the credit for this belongs not so much to the crew itself, as to the advent of Bruce Lee on to the silver screen. For Bruce could not only be idolized by girls in traditional terms as Supermale, his films demonstrated that the so-called weaker sex could master a technique which meant that they could fight on equal terms with boys – and win. Even if his girl fans didn't in practice follow the way of the dragon, Bruce Lee ratified their entry into the precincts of the fighting crew.

The traditions of the Martial arts imported from the Far East thus provided a new source of orientation, but not just for these crews. They appealed to larger sections of youth precisely because they spoke to a widespread sense of cultural displacement experienced during this period, 1972–4. In kung fu, kendo and karate, fighting technique is cultivated as an end in itself, a pure metaphysic of bodily control, split off from external reality, rather than what it had always been in the working class, a means of social control. In addition, the mass media intervened to blend all three elements, the native brawling tradition, youthful styles of aggro, and the martial arts, into a single *mise en scène* of contemporary violence.

There were no fighting crews on the Monmouth or Denby estates at this time (summer 1973). If there had been, then they would certainly have provided a 'solution' for lads like Bobby Munro. But the older fighting code still exerted an influence on most local youth, albeit at an increasing distance. The way Neil or Phil talked about fights or fighting was still a long way away from Micky Spyer's account. And those lads whose personal styles of aggro went over the limits were quickly isolated as 'nutters' and steered clear of as far as possible.

This did not mean that interest in karate and kung fu wasn't high. Many of the members of the Wall gang boasted of their prowess in such matters. But none showed any signs of expertise, or the inclination to submit themselves to the rigorous physical and mental discipline needed to acquire it. One night over the summer months, a group from the Wall went up the West End to see Bruce Lee in *Fist of Fury*. Afterwards, one of them attempted to emulate his new-found hero by chopping down a window.

Result: a cracked arm and seven stitches! The irony of the story is that the imagery of kung fu appeals most strongly to those kids who are often least equipped, in real terms, to master its techniques. The majority of the Wall, for example, had long since rejected the whole ethos of physical self-discipline and sustained effort which goes with success in organized sport.

The girls too had their stake in the martial arts. Since there was no fighting crew, they formed one of their own. This they modelled after the sixties bike gangs – a number of the lads were roaring around the estate on Suzukis at the time, and so provided the initial 'image' to emulate. The Denby Lady Hells Angels Club was formed. The girls didn't have bikes, of course, but they did have Bruce Lee, and they set off to practise their skills on the boys. There was nothing pretend about this. One lad was set on by a group of girls and so badly beaten up that he had to be sent to hospital. Needless to say, this aggro did nothing to alter the girls' fundamental one-down position in the local youth culture – as in other areas of their lives.

Enter the Dragon

In other words, the fascination of kung fu movies for these kids was not simply due to the fact that they presented a new and exotic fighting style. Their interest was much more sociological.

Bruce Lee in his movies finds himself, just as much as his fans in real life, caught up in a social system which he neither understands nor controls, because it is 'remote controlled' by superior, often institutional, forces, whose power is as hidden as it is all-pervasive. But unlike the heroes of the Western, gangster or fantasy stories (which in movie or comic form constitute these kids' staple cultural diet), Bruce Lee shuns the advanced weaponry of 'the Man' to fight back, just as he scorns ideological ruses. He takes on the technology of 'the system' armed with nothing but his fists, and his superior techniques of body control. And unlike these kids, he manages to salvage victory out of defeat.

The *mise en scène* of martial arts movies is, however, already familiar to the audience – from their comics and film-going, as much as from the narrative context of their everyday lives: rival mobs fighting over territory, plenty of ritual insults, even more physical injuries. For example, if we compare the narrative structure of *Fist of Fury* with the kids' own story-telling about the exploits and encounters they live through, we can see an almost point by point correspondence between the two. The story of *Fist of Fury* goes like this: The leader of the kung fu school has died. He has left behind a scroll of instructions on how his disciples are to carry on the tradition. It contains a key *interdict** – kung fu is to be used only in self-defence, and in the last resort when attacked. While the members of the school are pondering this, and their *lack of a leader* and how to replace him, in other words the *tasks* the founding father has *assigned* to them, they are interrupted by a visit of a 'mob' from a rival, Japanese school of martial arts. They have come not to praise the name of the dead master, but to *insult* him – and issue a challenge to his disciples to take them on in unarmed combat to see which of the two schools is superior. The elders hold to their master's instructions, and refuse to be provoked, so the Japanese leave, jeering at their cowardice, and taking with them the 'sacred text'. The kung fu school are in a dilemma. A *new task* has been *assigned* – to retrieve the scroll, but its *accomplishment* will inevitably mean *violating* the founder's *interdict*. They are caught in a *trap*. Young Bruce Lee rises to the challenge, even though he knows that it means banishment from the school. Alone and outcast, or rather since this is a movie with Hollywood pretensions, aided by an attractive young female accomplice who runs away from the school to join him, he succeeds in *avenging the insult* and retrieving the scroll. But this only brings further trouble from the Japanese mob, and the familar pattern of *attack* and *counter-attack* follows. In the process, Bruce Lee of course takes the place of the dead master, the school has found a *new leader*. But the authorities present them with an ultimatum: either Bruce Lee surrenders or the school is closed down. Bruce knows that he has successfully

* The italics indicate the narrative functions.

97

accomplished the task set by his dead teacher – the reputation and tradition of the kung fu school have been secured by his victories in battle – and will survive his own death. But if the school closes down everything he has fought for will be lost. So he gives himself up. And the school is left back where it was at the beginning of the story, *lacking a leader*.

The fascination of the content of such movies for working-class kids thus goes side by side with their unconscious recognition of its narrative style or 'grammar', as one which is identical with their own. They can read it effortlessly. Sometimes, at the level of motif, the links are more explicitly recognized, as in this poem written by a thirteen-year-old girl from Denby estate:

> *Tribute to Bruce Lee*
> When you were young, you used to roam
> the streets and alleys of Hong Kong
> You learn't your martial arts and then
> you tried it out on everywun.
>
> You led a gang or so they say
> and terrorized the town
> a rebel you will always be
> nowun can keep you down
>
> Your dead i know I've seen the proof
> your image still lives on
> you're worshipped now throughout the world
> even tho youre gone
>
> The waterfronts you used to go
> to fight and show your skill
> you always wun cos youre the guy
> nowun could ever kill
>
> You never thought of death i know
> cos death woud mean defeat
> and thats the thing you never knew
> how to win or beat.*

* This poem is not a bad bit of writing. But the standard of literacy or rather non-literacy revealed by a survey we carried out on 330 letters sent to a Bruce Lee fan mag (*Kung Fu Monthly*) was quite staggering. We estimated that the average 'literacy' age of the majority of these letter-writers was 10–

Enter the Dragon

In recent years there has been a lot of talk to the effect that violence in the mass media has produced the teenage rampage – working-class kids acting out the images and situations they see portrayed on the screen in real life. It should be clear from the analysis so far that what is in play is the linkage of two forms of 'collective representation' which have radically different historical origins and institutional supports. If the linkage is possible at all, it is because there is an objective correspondence between some oral traditions in working-class culture and *some* genres produced by the mass media. It is a correspondence of form, rather than content, and where it doesn't exist, the impact of the mass media on working-class consciousness is entirely negligible. Finally, both in the history of the class, and in the life history of those growing up into it, the narrative forms of oral culture predate those of the mass media and constitute a kind of permanent infra-structure, which condition and limit the effectivity of the latter.

The following discussion between two fourteen-year-old best mates living on the Monmouth may help to illustrate this. They are trying to reconstruct a subcultural past which they've experienced only at second hand, through the stories told by elder brothers or from what they've read in newspapers or books, or seen on TV or film. Images drawn from the mass media are

11 years. A readership survey of this magazine revealed the following profile:

Age: 7–14 17%, 15–21 69%, 21 and over 14%

Sex: Male 62%, Female 38%

Ethnic origins (*parents*): West Indian 31%, Asian 28%, Greek or other immigrant 18%, UK 27%

Social class (*parents*): Professional and Managerial 4%, Skilled manual/White collar 35%, Unskilled manual/White collar 61%

Total estimated readership of *Kung Fu Monthly*: 285,000.

This survey shows that a large majority of this audience were kids who for various reasons would be likely to experience the maximum difficulty in mastering techniques of literacy as taught in school; but because of their background they were likely to be highly sensitized to techniques of storytelling carried through the oral traditions of their own culture.

Configurations of Youth

inextricably interwoven with those drawn from real lives around the estate. But although they may be 'overdramatizing' this past, it is done with a self-critical awareness and no sentimentalism:

FRANK: Well, when I was young I used to really like the mods, but I couldn't stand the rockers. I thought they were a load of hooligans, you know. But as you grow older you kind of find out they was as bad as each other. I used to think of the rockers going round with chains and hatchets and things like that, but the mods used to go round just as much with bare fists. They'll just mob a couple of rockers, splatter them against the wall, rearrange their faces a little, and then the kid will go and get a couple of rockers to get the kids that got him and do exactly the same back . . .

TERRY: And when you was little, remember people used to come up and say 'who do you want, mods or rockers?' and there was two lots of gangs of us round here, one supported the rockers, and the other mods, and it just went on like that and there was fights over that.

FRANK: You know people used to reckon the teddy boys were the biggest, but the skins were thousands, tens of thousands all over Britain, and they were in the papers every day like the teds . . . Skins, bovver, all over the papers. Skins hit Brixton, Skins hit this, Skins hit that . . . there was a book out not long ago, you know it was really good, but it was a load of bollocks as well, if you know what I mean. It was called *Skinhead*. It was all about this geezer called Joe Hawkins and his mob and all the fights they used to have down Southend and all that. And after that he was sent to jail. And after he came out and became a suedehead and by the time you finished the book he was back in prison again for stabbing some Paki in the throat, with an umbrella, blood running all over him and that was that.

TERRY: It's like that film we see the other night, didn't we. *Heavy Traffic*. There was three greasers and they was trying to get this other kid to have it off with this bird, 'cos to become one you got to do it, you know, overnight, and anyway this kid doesn't know what to do, so they start mucking him about, hitting him over the head, and you see all the blood coming out, and they're pulling out chains and all sorts, and in the end they was all flaked out on the floor with half a leg missing here and there, and that. It was really tasty, but I don't think it's like that, 'cos me brother had a mate who was a greaser and he had a bike, you know, a big BMW, and he went on runs, the lot, but he never said anything about anything like that . . .

100

The Mary Whitehouse brigade would by now be getting quite excited picturing two young psychopathic thugs who set out each night to brutally translate these media fantasies into reality on whoever they can get their hands on. Concerned liberals may be worrying that these two lads are internalizing a 'stereotyped image of deviance', and acting up to *that*. The truth, however, is quite otherwise, and far more mundane.

Both Terry and Frank were popular members of the Wall fraternity, and well liked on the estate generally. Both their families were decidedly 'respectable' Irish, though not well off. Terry in particular had been an articulate supporter of the disco lobby described earlier. They both had a reputation locally as 'comedians' and in fact had quite a nice little double act going. They both knew how to 'handle themselves' and, for that reason, rarely got into fights. Equally, they'd both been in the odd bit of bother with the law, but only for trivial 'offences' to do with hanging about the Wall, and not involving violence of any kind. They didn't see themselves, and weren't seen by anyone else, as deviant, or as in any way different from the majority of the young people on the estate.

It becomes evident from this that such lads readily draw on the resources of the mass media where it supports their imaginative capacities as story-tellers of their own lives.

Sometimes there is an objective correspondence between situations portrayed in a given movie and the more subterranean realities of living in a 'hard' working-class area. In the following account, Terry draws on a media analogy to make the distinction – correctly from our own observations – between different roles in a well-known Islington fighting crew. But towards the end, media imagery spills out of its context and 'takes over the account'.

TERRY: . . . you usually find it's a dim bitch that's got all the bottle. If you look at *Clockwork Orange*, the one in there, he was dim, he had all the bottle there. You usually get that in crews . . . like we've got this kid, he's called Willy, he's as dim as they come, and every time there's a fight he don't care what the odds are, he just steams in, but then this other kid, they more or less take him for leader, Steve Taylor, when the fight starts off, he's usually at the back, he may be the best fighter there, but he's clever like. So it's the poor mugs blind at the front that gets the first chunk of lead and all their face just going splut all over the place and all you hear is chop chop and little groans and grunts, and little kids crawling out with half their jaws missing . . .

But this doesn't mean that Terry, Frank or any of the other lads have any difficulty in 'telling' fantasy from reality *when it matters*. The major subterranean tradition of violence in this part of London was carried on by the fraternity of professional villains whose base was in the Cross Keys pub opposite the Black Horse. The local lads' attitude to these men was nothing if not ambivalent. They admired their trappings of affluence, the expensive suits, cars and the rest, and the fact that they had got this without having to work. But the other trappings of their trade, the scars, the broken noses, their justified reputation for calculated violence, the spells in prison, this inspired only fear. They might watch at a safe distance, but they didn't aspire to be any part of it.

FRANK: But then you get these really hard nuts, about twenty and up. You know, there's really big fights. Like we were up the hospital the other day, and this geezer come in, he works up the Riverside,* and he's been slashed across the face and he's been stabbed twice in the back by some other geezer from another mob, reckoned he should have the job or something, so he puts him out of commission like. I think that's pretty stupid, you know, but if any of that lot are around, the kids stand around like little goody boys . . .

In fact these kids have a very solid, and material sense of their own reality – and it is from that base-line that they criticize its distortion and misrepresentations by press and TV. For example, another lad, in his early twenties, a keen Arsenal supporter but now grown out of the North Bank, comments on a TV discussion programme in which a panel of experts have given their views on the nature and causes of contemporary teenage violence:

Well there was this geezer sitting there who thought he knew all

* As described later in this section, the newly opened Riverside Sports Centre recruited a number of local professional 'hard men' to police the place after repeated fights and vandalism. As this story reveals, there was some 'competition' for the job among the fraternity.

about it, but he didn't know nothing if you ask me . . . He was going on about soccer hooligans and how they carry on down the ends, and he says, well, it's all because they don't like the middle classes taking over the game, getting in the act like. Well, anyone who ever been down the North Bank'll tell you they don't give a sod for the students and all the other wankers and pooftas that turn up. They never go down the end anyway, they're too scared. All the North Bank care about is their team and the other end and that's all there is to it.

The Great Chinese Take-Away Massacre

One incident which was recounted in numerous versions by Monmouth and Denby kids during the time of the Black Horse disco came to be known as the Great Chinese Take-Away Massacre. The following is a synopsis of these accounts:

One evening, after they came out of the pub, a group of Black Horse regulars went down to the Chinese take-away on the main road. After getting their food, they were standing outside, talking and laughing, when a squad car pulled up. A young police constable jumped out and pushed his way through the lads to Brian, who was in the centre of the group. The P.C. told Brian to Break it Up and Move On as they were causing an obstruction. Brian replied to the effect that he didn't know eating chop suey in the street was against the law. At which, with the ceremonial utterance 'don't get clever with me, you Irish bastard, I'm having you, you're nicked', the constable proceeded to bundle Brian into the car. The rest of the group crowded round, jeering. Two other young policemen got out, smacked a couple of the boys in the mouth, and grabbed a third and bundled him too into the car, which then sped off, leaving the survivors to elaborate the more or less heroic nature of the encounter to themselves and their mates.

They didn't do what middle-class youths might have done in similar circumstances and what advocates of children's rights advocate – namely, become morally outraged at the injustice they had suffered. It didn't occur to them to go round to the police station to make a complaint, for example, or to write a letter to their M.P. or to the local paper or to the N.C.C.L. This has nothing to do with their lack of the communication skills which such strategies imply. Rather these boys have an implicit awareness of their specific class position *vis-à-vis* authority. The rule here is that you try and steer clear of the law if you can, but at the same time you don't let the law dictate what you should or should not do. If you or your mates get nicked, then that's it. It's a fairly routine fact of life, and there's nothing you can do about it.

The first thing to notice about such street encounters between kids and the police is that at one level both sides start from the *same* rules in the *same* context and recognize the fact that they share a common code as members of the same culture. Consider the following account by a fourteen-year-old boy from the Denby estate:

We was walking down the road, me and my mate, we were just talking to each other and because this copper had nothing to do, he wanted to try and get us up the old bill, and he said we was taking the mick out of him, and he was, you know, like a flash copper. And my mate, he's looking at the copper and giving him bad looks, and then the copper takes his helmet off and says 'Go on then, hit me' and my mate's dying to hit him but he knows if he did, the copper could get him nicked, and then the copper goes, 'I'll take the lot of you on in the garage.' But what could we do? We couldn't, could we? Then we've had it, haven't we?

There are no ambiguities of recognition in this account; it's a meeting between, not strangers, but positionally known enemies. The issue is 'Who rules round here?' Such encounters are always prestructured in terms of rules of territoriality, and unfold in the form of a street challenge between two rival mobs. In this account we can see the classic sequence of ritual insult taking place; the initial informative-performative bind (taking the mick), the exchange of looks, the invitation to physical injury. The immediate pretext of the incident is, however, explained here in terms of the copper's boredom on the beat. This is not just a projection on the lad's part; it corresponds to sociological fact. Young police officers not only get bored on the beat but respond, just like any other working-class lad, by an intervention designed to generate a consequential narrative event. Often it is not only a question of getting into the action and having something to report but, where an arrest ensues, getting off the beat and getting back to the warmth and comfort of the station (not to mention an additional perk of the following morning off to appear in court). Late at night and in bad weather the temptation must be irresistible. Drunks, unlicensed street traders, and footloose kids provide the stock in trade for the policeman on walkabout or panda patrol.

So what began as a ritual exchange between 'equals' quickly escalates into a highly unequal confrontation between one mob, which has the full weight of the State apparatus behind it, and the other which has only each other. Magistrates' courts, borstal, detention centre – these institutions are all too visible in the mind's eye of the kids, from either their own past experiences or those represented by mates or relatives. The copper, however, acts *as if* this was not true, as if these institutions did not exist, and all that was happening was a fight between equals. He symbolizes this by taking off his helmet – his badge of office. Needless to say the kids aren't conned – they'd like to have a go, but they know that if they do they've 'had it'. In fact the 'fair deal' the copper is proposing is nothing of the sort, as both sides are fully aware. If these lads do square up and succeed in beating the copper in a 'fair fight' – a somewhat unlikely outcome since they are two pint-sized fourteen-year-olds against a six-foot fourteen-stone full-grown man – then next day they are very likely to find themselves up in court charged with assault, or worse. The alternative is to take a beating, and even then there is no guarantee that they won't be arrested into the bargain, although it is much less likely. The only other solution – the one these boys opted for – was to back down, apologize, or in some other way extricate themselves. Every way, they lose. But for some kids, like Brian, and in some encounters, like the Great Chinese Take-Away

Massacre, it is actually *less* humiliating to be arrested than to suffer the indignity of being beaten up or of backing down.*

* Encounters such as those described above were a common experience for kids in this part of North London, and we listened to many accounts similar to those just quoted. To try to check their frequency we asked four members of the popular Wall hangout opposite the Black Horse to keep a record over four weeks of the occasions on which they were stopped by the police. Two of them had court convictions for minor offences, the other two didn't. One was a fringe member of the Wall, two were regulars, and one we judged to be 'hard core'. We should stress that none of these kids had a hard delinquent status in the area; they all had relatively well-paid jobs, and one in fact was going to evening class twice a week to qualify for an apprentice-ship.

There were fifteen separate incidents recorded over the period. Ten of them took place in situations where they were with mates, including each other. Eight took place after ten p.m. In only two cases were boys lawbreaking in any recognizable form. Once they were caught joy-riding in a relative's car. The other instance concerned a pub fight when the police were called. The remaining incidents all took place in the context of street challenge: either on the Wall itself (5), or outside cinemas, cafés and other youth hangouts (7), or when just walking about (3).

All this might be expected. But in comparing the experiences of the four lads there is a surprise: there was no appreciable difference in either the frequency or the seriousness of encounters between the two lads known to the police and those who were not. Nor did their degree of involvement in the Wall fraternity seem to make a difference. There seemed to be a fairly equal and random distribution of incidents. Obviously this has a lot to do with the short time-span of this piece of research, and may be something of an 'optical illusion'. If this kind of getting into trouble is situationally determined, we should expect that the stronger and hence longer a kid's commitment to the Wall, the more likely that routine, random police harass-ment would be registered in terms of court appearances and convictions. So over a longer period of research, differences between the lads might begin to show, if not necessarily in any predictable way. But what it also points to is that it is essential to distinguish the kind of processes which determine degree of commitment to the Wall, from the mechanisms which produce a young 'apprentice gangster' of the Billy Sheahan variety. There are cases in which these two may mesh in, but they are likely to be the exception rather than the rule.

Kill the Bill

('Kill, Kill, Kill the Bill', North Bank Arsenal chant)

At times, it seems, at least from media reports, that the day-to-day crux of violence in many areas of Britain is the confrontation between 'hooligans', 'vandals', and other kinds of 'delinquent' youth and the police. Both sides have their public defenders: each is accused of provocation and wilful brutality, with the police public relations office coming out on top. But the underlying logic of this is rarely brought to light.

The confrontation itself has been going on for over a century. From the first report of the Society for Investigating the Causes of the Alarming Increase of Juvenile Delinquency in the Metropolis, published in 1816, to the current outpourings of the youth research industry, sections of working-class youth have been seen as a natural obstacle to the maintenance of 'Public order and social progress'. Whether they clung to elements of a pre-industrial culture to resist the new work disciplines of industrial capitalism, rebelled against consignment to a condition of wageless dependence and subsequent marginality in the labour market, or improvised forms of urban recreation which failed to match up to the prevailing notions of bourgeois rationality, generation after generation of youth have been at the centre of a single and continuous public debate. Its idioms may have changed over a hundred years but its essential terms of reference have not.

Working-class kids of course have taken no part in the debate; it has gone on not just under their noses but over their heads, because it is essentially an argument between two sections of the upper middle class – between the liberals, the politicians of conscience whose theme is 'give youth a chance', and the conservatives, the defenders of law and order who reply with 'give society a chance'. Despite the accusations of infidelity flying to and fro, both partners have derived a certain strength from the marriage; the first the *force* of its categorical imperatives; the second its *illusion* of political neutrality, of rising majestically above the sordid interests of class and State power. The debate on juvenile delinquency has played its part in cementing the marriage as well as perpetuating the quarrel; were its causes to be found in the individual or society? Were its remedies reform or punishment?

But this relationship is far from being simply platonic – although the dialogue can still be seen taking place today in the pages of the *Daily Telegraph* or *New Society*. It consummated itself *materially* through a specific institution. The development of the modern police force was of course a response to the crisis in urban administration which occurred in early Victorian Britain. An 'old' state apparatus confronted new relations of reproduction thrown up by industrial capitalism, and created new sources of class tension in the expanding towns and cities, even if this was often expressed in traditional, pre-capitalist forms. In resolving this crisis the new force became the principal agent of *both* moral *and* juridical ideologies. These were to be combined as a new *practice* of policing which would cohere them into a single system of rules of public order, uniformly defined, and implemented.

This has put the British police force in the peculiar situation of having to combine two distinct and contradictory functions: first, as agents of a moral ideology represented in terms of a neutral, and purely '*expressive*' function of 'community welfare' – helping old ladies across the road, giving directions to strangers, finding lost children or pets, rescuing people from floods, fires and the other emergencies of everyday life; and second, as agents of the dominant political and economic interests (private property, etc.) which are protected by the judicial and penal system, an explicitly *repressive* function which involves them in attacking picket lines, harassing dissident groups or other minority interests, breaking up demonstrations, and so on. Police public relations, of course, continually emphasizes the first role, exemplified in 'Dixon of Dock Green', to the exclusion of the second, or rather presents the second as a 'natural' extension of the first. If this manoeuvre is possible, and largely successful, it is because of the special relation between the two sides of the police's job.

In theory, and mostly in practice, Dixon of Dock Green performs his welfare function, impartially, throughout society, irrespective of the class, colour or creed of the recipients of his services. This comes from the fact that historically the police, along with social workers, have *confiscated* certain routine functions of mutual aid in working-class communities and institutionalized them as a professional agency of social control, imposed from outside through the state apparatus. It is in this way that the moral ideology of one class is imposed on another in a context where there only appear to be 'classless' individual citizens-in-need-or-distress.

But it is a different story with the other side of the job, which is to search and destroy classes or groups who are seen as 'dangerous' or in some way a threat to the established political, moral and economic order. The result is that experience of police behaviour differs between the classes, in a rather less than obvious way. People in middle-class residential areas directly experience *only* the welfare aspects of police work, and have no difficulty in perceiving the job of protection of the institutions of private property, including of course their own homes, as a natural extension of this. With the evidence of their own eyes, they daily bear witness to the illusion of the unity of the police force's role. Against this, people in working-class districts experience police behaviour in full contradiction with itself – since they are the recipients of both expressive and repressive attentions. In some neighbourhoods this may go even further; where there is a strong sense of social cohesion and mutual aid, plus a developed moral order which is strongly antagonistic to middle-class values, people will call on the welfare resources of the police only in the last resort, and then rarely.

In consequence, no amount of evidence that the police fabricate charges, beat up suspects, or harass kids on the street, as a routine part of their job, is likely to convince residents of well-to-do neighbourhoods; any more than you can convince black kids in Brixton that the police spend a good part of their time doing useful things like helping old ladies across the road. And split perception in turn gives rise to a whole spectrum of statements about the police – from 'all coppers are bastards' through 'there's some good coppers and some bad' to 'British police are the best in the world'.

It is important to realize, though, that the structural contradiction in the position of the British police force is registered within the force itself as divisions and conflicts between its various branches. Rivalries between the boys in blue and plain clothes men. Between local station staff and élite cadres like the Special Patrol Group, Regional Crime Squads, Special Branch, which are peripatetic, and come into a local manor only to 'sort it all out'. In that sense the contradiction is contained within the boundaries of the institution itself and its professional ideology.

There is one section of the force, and one context of policing, in which the contradiction is not only not contained, but more or less dramatically acted out day by day: the uniformed beat coppers who patrol the streets of working-class areas, on foot or in cars, are in a situation where they have to show both 'faces' simultaneously, especially in confronting those kids who have already staked out a rival claim to the 'freedom of the streets'. In the area covered by Monmouth and Denby estates, for example, the home beat copper, Constable Groves, worked in the local Shore Street Youth Centre in his spare time, knew many of the teenagers by their first names, and used the knowledge he gained informally about their delinquent activities to get them arrested. He rarely arrested them in person, merely passed the information on to the CID. Quite a few of the kids sussed on to the situation. His presence in the youth club may have had a deterrent effect, though not the one intended – it simply deterred many from going near the place! Constable Groves himself had no qualms of conscience about the matter, he saw no contradiction, his professional ideology saw to that. Or perhaps it would be fairer to say that, through this ideology, he saw the contradiction in a different light.

All working-class coppers start on the beat: that is, at the bottom of the career pyramid. If the beat copper is ambitious, or corrupt, or both, he will want to get out of uniform and into a plain clothes job as quickly as possible – that is where the status and the easy pickings are. But no copper gets promoted off the beat for being good at finding lost kids or helping old ladies across the road! If you are good at that, then that is where you will stay, as an advertisement for police public relations. Promotion is geared to productivity, that is arrests, and local youth are simply the easiest available source of arrests. Constable Groves's dilemma was this: he liked the area, he had grown up there, and in a strange kind of way he liked the kids; at the same time, he did not want to spend the rest of his life on the beat. So he effected a compromise. He made sure that he was responsible for a certain quota of local arrests, enough to keep the local station happy and his own promotion prospects alive, but not so many that he alienated the local community, or made his own position within it socially untenable. But it was an uneasy compromise at best. (This has been based on informal conversations with Constable Groves. His own analysis is, however, confirmed by sociological studies of the British police force.)

Where do the kids themselves stand in this? We could say that if they are victimized routinely by local police it is because the force itself is trapped in the contradiction inscribed in its historical origins. The paradox goes like this: if and when working-class youth exert a presence outside contexts of social control (family, school, work), this is transfigured into the problematic of 'juvenile delinquency' by a public debate in which they are seen either as morally at risk (that is a risk to themselves) or as a risk to the law and order of society. But the gentleman's agreement to differ which rules this debate is perpetually threatened by the nature of relationship between the police who are meant to embody its resolution and the kids who are supposed to be the cause. There is a permanent tendency for the police to behave, and to be seen by large sections of the population, as a purely repressive instrument of class domination. Hence the structural necessity of developing a second force, parallel to the police, which could shore up the moral side of the delinquency equation.

Historically this role was played by the great reforming voluntary agencies thrown up during the heroic phase of liberal imperialism. Today it is largely played by the probation service, the youth service, local authority welfare departments and other agencies financed from public funds. This army of social workers have sometimes been called the soft cops. Usually this is taken to imply that in some way they collude with police, magistracy, penal system and so on, or otherwise pursue similar strategies of social control by subtler, less overtly repressive means. Sometimes this is indeed the case. But increasingly social workers see their role in terms of protecting kids from being railroaded into punitive institutions by the forces of law and order. Even and especially when they do this, they function as a kind of loyal opposition, which unwittingly allows the 'hard cop' to preserve the credibility of their Dixon of Dock Green image while continuing to harass the kids. The collusion between hard and soft cops thus works at a deeper and more unconscious level. Both are required to preserve the equilibrium of the delinquency debate, just as both combine to produce its material evidence – i.e. the 'delinquents' – to support it. Working-class kids are therefore used to integrate a theoretical ideology (the delinquency debate) with a set of ideological practices (police and social work) *and* to harmonize a conflict between two sections of another class. The whole problematic is basically alien to them, and runs counter to their own definition of the situation; the most intense socialization, over an extended period of time, is needed before these kids will learn to mis-recognize their situation in terms of juvenile delinquency. Only a minority, categorized as recidivists, ever do.

If it is *working-class* kids who are subjected to all this, then this is not because of some political conspiracy against them by the establishment; middle-class kids may not of course routinely get into confrontations with the police, and when they do 'cause trouble' they may be dealt with more leniently, or in other ways. But that is essentially beside the point. The real issue is that the whole edifice of delinquency is sustained by routine confrontations on the streets of working-class neighbourhoods, between working-class kids and young working-class beat coppers. And if it is working-class *kids* who are involved, then this has less to do with the psychodynamic of adolescence than with their structural position in the political geography of the working-class community.

All the evidence points to the fact that this is a struggle which neither 'side' can ever finally win. The police never win their 'fight against juvenile crime'; increased police activity results only in higher juvenile crime figures, so the problem appears to get worse, not better, and it never goes away, any more than the kids do. Equally, all the rehabilitation, training and therapy programmes appear to have little or no effect; detention centres, community homes and borstals produce more kids officially classified as recidivists and hardened young offenders than they do model citizens. But if the statutory agencies are 'fighting a losing battle', then it is not because the kids are winning; as we have seen, they are permanently fighting a rearguard action. We have tried to analyse some of the structures of constraint which determine and continually reproduce this stalemate. In focusing on the routine, typically street encounter between forces of law and public order and kids in our working-class neighbourhoods, we looked at how the real relations of both to the state apparatus are lived out by them as a system of *imaginary* relations.

These relations are imaginary not in the sense that they are illusory, but in that they enfold the human beings who find themselves in confrontation in a common misrecognition of the real mechanism which have distributed them to their respective positions. It is rather like a fight arranged between two boxers representing clubs which have a long-standing feud. The referee is there to see fair play, but both go into the ring determined to nail their opponent by any means to hand. The lighter of the two is relying on his quickness to tire his bigger opponent out, while the latter is counting on his rabbit punch to settle matters. However, the promoters have rigged the fight. While as promoters they may profit from staging the spectacle itself, it is against their interest to let things get out of control. The spectators might decide to join in and then they'd have a riot on their hands. So both fighters have been trained by a special method to box their own shadows. They have been told that this is the best, indeed only permitted, way to fight, and this is the only way they have learnt how. So when the fight starts they spend the whole time trying to nail each other's shadows. Now and then, almost by accident, one or other of them manages to land a real punch to the body, just often enough to keep the crowd in their seats, but not often enough to ensure a knock-out decision. As the fight proceeds, both boxers get increasingly frustrated, tired and wild in their aim, but neither can unlearn their shadow-boxing technique, or get sufficiently to grips with their adversary to settle the issue one way or the other, once and for all. The referee declares himself the winner, the crowd goes home, the followers of the two camps neither triumphant nor enraged, but alike arguing about the result and demanding a return match, while the promoters quietly pocket the takings.

But analogy is not homology. There has been no shortage of those who have seen the issue of delinquency and social control as an epicentre of class struggle, or at least a highly dramatic symptom of it, especially in periods of economic boom, when the traditional point of confrontation, in production, seems relatively quiescent. There are those who urge youngsters to organize against the police – to understand that the fight is rigged and attack the referee. And there are others who try and get them to join legal workshops, learn their rights, and the language of the referee, so as to fight more effectively. In both cases, the attempt is made to get kids to reinterpret their position, to account for their experiences through alternative codes, whether this be the universalism of revolutionary rhetoric, or legal bureaucratic expertise. There is little evidence, however, that either of these approaches has been very successful. The young 'victims of class justice' have largely stood their own cultural ground. But perhaps the strategic issue is not how to get them to switch codes, but to switch the context of confrontation. Away from the street and into the institutions where the real relations of production and reproduction, which determine their lives, continue to seep through the imaginary. The workplace and the juvenile market. The family and the system of domestic labour. The school and

114

the education of labour power. This certainly involves a shift in consciousness; and a retreat from unmediated encounters with local police, an advance to more organized positions within the institutions which act through them. This is not something which it seems can best be negotiated from the street itself, or from some interstitial base which replicates its functions. The real conditions lie in the co-ordinates of a political geography, which at present maps the interest groupings of youth into a space of powerlessness and polarity. The co-ordinates are those of the local parent cultures, and the adult labour movement. The real struggle is to open up an effective space of youth representation at this level.

Black and White

On the Monmouth and Denby many tenants were busy pressing for even greater police surveillance of their youngsters. Yet it was noticeable how the organizations of the local black community, small and isolated as it was, tended to back up the kids in their frequent clashes with the police, often in the face of parental opposition. Uhuru, a black youth and community centre adjoining the estate, often took up complaints of police harassment and made representations on their members' behalf. Uhuru was associated with the Black Freedom and Unity Party, and its programme emphasized the values of black nationalism and encouraged the manifestation of black culture. They had a clear orientation to youth. The leader saw the job of the centre as a place where the different positions taken up by black youth, from apprentice hustler, thrown out on to the street by a disapproving family, to aspiring night-school student aiming at a white-collar job, could find a common ground, in a black political culture 'which excluded both lumpen and petit bourgeois solutions.' The kids responded by exuding a strong sense of pride in the place, and in being black.

The local white tenants looked on. 'If the blacks run their own community centre, why can't we?' Many felt unwarrantedly threatened. It only took one occasion when a procession of black

115

youngsters, dressed as freedom fighters, wound its way in proud style through the gleaming maisonettes of Cambria, Snowdon and Caerphilly, for rumour to do the rest. A move was made to get Uhuru closed down. Stories of wild all-night parties, rubbish overflowing into the street and so on gained wide circulation. The organizers of Uhuru looked on this, as on other attempts by whites to 'organize', with weary contempt.

As we stated earlier, there was a history of Irish – Black hostilities as these two immigrant cultures faced each other across the public bar of the old Black Horse. And neither side was averse to putting a bit of emphasis into settling arguments. This in turn rubbed off on the attitudes of local youth. On one occasion, we proposed a visit by members of the Wall to Uhuru's to film one of their karate training sessions. High initial enthusiasm, of course, but more about karate than Uhuru's.

We arrived one summer evening to find our 'clients' in their usual station by the Cross Keys. 'We're off to the black youth centre. You coming?' Embarrassed silence. One or two of the group detach themselves and start to melt away into the shadows. 'What about you, Doughnut?' 'What, me? Go in there with all those jungle bunnies?' Looks to mates for support. His mates solidarize with a chorus of racist repartee. More Wall habitués melt into the shadows. Until finally we are left with the vociferous Doughnut, his mate Greek Angelo, and their girls. We appeal to the girls, who seem quite keen to make the visit. Doughnut: 'If you go in there with those jungle bunnies, then don't bother to speak to me again.' All this was going on in the presence of a young West Indian boy who lived on Denby, hung out on the Wall with the rest, and was close mates with quite a few. A split perception. They might call him Sambo to his face, but 'he's OK, he's one of us'.

So the refusal of the Monmouth boys to visit Uhuru had a more complex rationale than simple racial prejudice. As we tried to show earlier, the breakdown of any stable subcultural identity of their own, coupled with the erosion of many of the traditional supports of the parent culture, meant that they felt particularly threatened by the presence of any cohesive socio-cultural grouping. This was what the black kids at Uhuru represented. Moreover, black youth had already wrested the title of hardest fighters around from their Irish predecessors – and precisely by mastering the superior techniques of unarmed combat which the Wall could emulate only in fantasy. The notion of entering black territory armed with nothing more than a video camera broke all known rules. It could be seen as nothing but a prelude to humiliation. The presence of the girls further complicated the issue. To have to show up their lack of expertise in the martial arts, in front of them, was the final insult. Still less did they want to reveal their wider apprehensions.

Over the whole summer period before the opening of the disco in the Black Horse there were to be a series of further stand-offs between the black and white youth of the area. The most popular disco in this part of the borough was the 2-4-8. Housed in the huge shell of an old church, quite the opposite to the small, intimate club popular in the sixties, it attracted kids from all over Highbury and Islington. Under soaring Gothic arches the big beat boomed out. In the semi-darkness, patrons would alternately mill about, sit in discreet rows along the walls or hang out in groups. It was the big dance halls of the thirties and forties, only here you could enjoy moments of intimacy as well as feeling part of something larger. Inevitably, 2-4-8 became one of the main arenas where teenage geopolitics were acted out. The *invasion* of the disco by teams of blacks from Holloway during this summer, and their *success* in establishing a *dominant* presence, prompted strong reactions:

It's really packed out with coons, really bad, and every time you walk down there, you're mugged. And they don't hit you or nothing, they just threaten you. They would turn you over, frisk you down, all for your money and that, and so, you know, people got a bit sick of it. In the end we told our mates and they're all about 18, so all the whites went, and [the blacks] used to go down the disco and used to take it over. So [the whites] went and waited one night and they knew there was going to be a lot of them down there because [the blacks] used to take over the place, so they just went down . . .

Such attempts to improvise a white solidarity continually came up against the fragmented and dispersed consciousness prevailing amongst them at this time. This in stark contrast to the blacks. As one Irish lad put it:

> A fight starts off between a white and a coloured, the whites, they don't clan with one another, so they just stand round and watch unless it's his mate; but you get these other ones, they come steaming in, the coons, and they're kicking the poor kids all over the place . . . If you have a fight with one coloured kid, he goes and pulls over about 70 coloureds and they're all around you and you can't really fight back because what's going to happen to you?

This account was checked by our own observations, over two years, of this and similar 'racially integrated' youth clubs in North London. The general relation of forces between black and white followed very much the pattern if not the detail depicted above. The conclusion must be that any simple strategy aimed at creating some kind of unmediated unity between the two 'sides' is pure political wish-fulfilment. In Part Three of this book we shall show how this is a situation which is exploitable by the National Front and similar groups.*

* In the last years, 1974/7, there have been signs that the situation of black youth, in this part of London at least, has changed. From the outside it seems that there is a growing mood of disaffiliation from the kind of involvements represented by Uhuru and similar organizations, and a move towards highly personalized idioms of expression through the media of fashion, music, argot. In other words, style cultivated as an end in itself seems to have replaced the popular memory of political struggle as the prime source of self-imagery. Equally, they seem to be less socially cohesive. There has been an increasing incidence of infighting, often on a territory basis, coupled with sporadic offensives against white youth. Only commentators within the black community can say whether this does in fact represent a full-scale retreat from the positions of the political subculture established between 1967 and 1971, and a drift into deviance. But it seems dangerous to conclude, as some have done, that black kids are making a conscious political choice to drop out of the educational system and labour market.

Back at the Youth Club

Although as we have seen there was a demand for a disco in the Black Horse, this doesn't mean that there wasn't any youth provision for the neighbourhood. There was. The Shore Street Youth Centre had serviced the needs of several generations. It was housed in an old board school, a gaunt impregnable building. Long echoing corridors, winding stone staircases, tiled walls. It had been built to contain even the most violent onslaughts of its young inmates, and it had succeeded. With the establishment of the statutory youth service after the war, many such old schools had been taken over. Attempts were constantly being made to refurbish these forbidding environments, to dispel forever the associations of school drill and exercise yard. But in the case of Shore Street, a new coat of paint and the latest line in youth service furnishings just weren't enough. Outside, the entrance was still guarded by the faded insignia of an earlier dual morality. BOYS. GIRLS. Such relics of the past might have been an embarrassment to the administrators but of course were ignored by the kids. Disco nights, however, required some imagination to transform the old gym, with its wall bars and indoor netball pitch, into an intimate haven of local night life.

The warden of Shore Street, Jock, was a local man, and one of the old school. Hard but fair. 'You can have a laugh with him, but if you muck about he comes down on yer' – that was the general consensus amongst the membership. Everything that could be 'shifted' in Shore Street was either nailed down or under lock and key. Jock carried all the keys with him in a huge bunch, and wherever he went it was 'Can I have the keys to this, can I have the keys to that'. Jock took a special pride in his ability to control his manor, and he had able support in the form of Constable Groves, his second in command.

The view from behind Jock's desk: head round the door. One of the instructors. Heard anything about those new bar bells? . . . I've been waiting for weeks . . . the lads are going on about it. Phone call to head office. What to do about the fifty hat-stands just dumped in the club by a cynical ILEA driver. The YO thought they might come in useful, but where to store them? Enter lad holding out broken table tennis bat. That's your third this week. What do you do, eat 'em? Jack was far from being a desk-bound penpusher. He saw his job as 'an uphill fight' to instil the values of self-respect, team spirit, and the traditional boys' club ethos in the centre.

Jock and his colleagues worked under an enthusiastic Area Youth Officer, Helmut Klein. Klein enjoyed the reputation of being both supportive to his staff and enthusiastic about the importance of youth work itself (youth as the future). In Klein's view, nothing is too good when it comes to providing facilities for the kids; what is needed above all is more money 'so that we can have more clubs and facilities and more kids making use of them'. Klein had no particular evangelical axe to grind, however. He supported the 'revolutionaries' of Uhuru as determinedly as he supported the 'conservatives' of Shore Street, as long as what was provided in these places was beneficial for the kids and protected them from more harmful influences or the disease of boredom. In fact Klein himself saw youth work as non-political, non-ideological. 'The kids come first.'

As part of the wider process of gentrification in this part of North London there had been an influx of young professionals, many of them fresh from teacher training colleges and university sociology departments, enthusiastic to apply their skills and ideals to local needs. They found Helmut Klein receptive to their approach.

These were people whose instinctive rejection of authoritarian structures during their student days had been fuelled by a gamut of radical alternatives. From anti-psychiatry to de-schooling, from women's liberation to street theatre. Now they attempted in their different ways to put their theories into practice. There followed a series of initiatives in local youth provision which went beyond the traditional bounds of the youth club, just as it attracted the otherwise unclubbables. Adventure playgrounds, drop-in places with names like the Shack, the Hut, detached youth work with the fighting crews. And the Steelyard Free School.

The free school was Council-backed and supported by progressive middle-class elements in the ruling labour group. The parent culture was less enthusiastic. The school was seen realistically as an opposition force, and this 'prejudice' was shared by local working-class politicians.

The Steelyard was a ramshackle collection of old workmen's huts and long stone sheds scattered amidst vast expanses of disused railway land. On this urban frontier land a kind of duplicate of the street hangout outside appeared to prevail. Bundles of kids of all ages could be seen rushing about together in the rubble, tinkering with car engines, riding bikes and scooters, or embarking on the odd bit of clearance and repainting. Unlike the street, however, young men and women, in their early twenties for the most part, could be seen running alongside them. Again unlike the street, the 'teachers' would frequently be called on to initiate activities, instruct as to the art of motor-cycle maintenance, or lead the charge on some old bus that needed to be reduced to scrap. The Steelyard would echo constantly to the cry of 'Jeff! Jeff!' as the kids would search high and low for their headmaster and substitute gang leader, without whom they would grow curiously lost and sedentary. Even the desire to muck about came hard, and individual patterns of boredom and loneliness would break through. The twenty or so Steelyard regulars tended to be children who, despite whatever personal qualities they may have had, could make it neither at school nor in the street gang. Many of them had refused school and drifted to the Steelyard not so much because they hated lessons as because they hated getting picked on or getting into fights in the playground. In compensation they got an alternative gang.

The Steelyard held little appeal to the vast majority of schoolchildren, not even those resistant truants for whom it was designed. As Billy Sheahan, an ace truant, once put it, 'It's not a real school, they don't learn yer nothing there.' Steelyarders were characterized by Billy as 'Odds and sods, you get all kinds, all colours', that is, a bunch of loners, with no gang pull.

The Steelyard was not so much a free school as a fall-out shelter existing beyond the reach of parents, cops and headmasters. Unlike some such schools, little attention was paid to formal education. But in providing a safe hangout above all else, the Steelyard had become just another ghetto for disaffiliated kids. Indeed, the sense of displacement from the parent culture felt by some kids on the Wall was actually being reinforced and institutionalized in the Steelyard.

This kind of intervention was supported by a more informal movement taking place at this time in the neighbourhood. The arrival of a large group of squatters, advocates of alternative housing and domestic relations, had considerable impact. For the squatters brought with them a strongly developed life-style and social network, elements that were missing from the lives of quite a few teenagers. And in some cases fascination gave way to active involvement.

For example, two sixteen-year-old best mates, who had been prominent members of the Wall, gradually severed contact, preferring instead the freewheeling atmosphere of the hippy household. Both Jacko and Pete had creative ambitions which had been effectively blocked by their class position. Pete had been in a Boys Brigade band which had nurtured the musical talents he was now devoting to emulating Jimi Hendrix, rather than J. P. Souza. He had a discriminating knowledge of popular music, preferring progressive rock and soul, and within this genre he had considered views for and against particular artists. He reserved his special contempt for mainstream 'Top of the Pops'.* He was working in a supermarket, but his real ambition was to be a professional musician. Jacko's concern was more with the plastic arts. He had worked as a commercial sign writer, and had developed an interest in typography, graphic design, and from there painting. He might be working as a packer in a warehouse, but his sights were set on art school. But he had none of the required O-levels, and

* This was in sharp contrast to the majority of local kids, whose musical interests were largely dictated by 'Top of the Pops', a diffuse mixture of idioms and genre, synthetically blended together. Their preference for a particular record, for example, was in terms of either its danceability or the persona of the pop star; no aesthetic criteria intrinsic to music were allowed to break into the more generalized schema of youth culture.

the prospect of two years' evening class was just too daunting.

It is easy to see why these two found the company of the young squatters, many of them students or middle-class 'drop-outs', more congenial to their aspirations than that of their mates on the Wall. Still, the more deviant aspects of life in the hippy household, in sex matters and drug-taking, they both found more than somewhat alarming. Help was at hand, however. The adventure playground workers had strong social as well as ideological links with the squatters. Jacko and Pete graduated from hanging about the squats, listening to sounds and eating macrobiotic food, to a crudely defined position as co-youth-workers on the adventure playground. Here was a renewed source of legitimacy and social status in their own community. This was a development which defeated the analytics of their former mates on the Wall, who saw only the end (respectable status and special quasi-adult privileges) and not the means, and tended to consign them unfairly to the category of 'tamoes'.

Such transformations were not simply confined to individual histories or to isolated experiments, they were also proceeding within established youth service provision. Back at the Shore Street Centre, Jock, retiring early, was replaced by Ray Andrews, a young man with a definite hippy presence and a marked antipathy to the 'boys' club' approach.

For some weeks Andrews worked in an uneasy partnership with Jock's old second in command, Constable Groves. As we've mentioned before, Groves enjoyed his voluntary work with the local lads; 'there's a bit of me that wants to be running around wild in the evenings, I suppose,' is how he put it, but 'you've got to lay down the law with them, draw a line, and say here's how far you can go and no further.'

This approach was anathema to Andrews. He called a meeting of members and staff and informed them that there were no longer any official club rules. From now on there would be a 'democratic' set-up: a free and happy atmosphere; the development of personal relationships was of a higher priority for the centre now than how many sports trophies it collected. With Groves looking on in amazement, Andrews initiated group

123

encounter sessions for members and staff. Everybody was encouraged to sit around in a circle and hold hands, with eyes closed, touch each other and so on (a group therapy strategy known as 'the truth game', which aims to develop non-verbal communication as the basis of authentic relationships). In this tough mainstream youth club, Andrews tried in effect to collapse the social distances that separated working-class kids and a middle-class adult by relaxing techniques of body control. But, while Andrews rolled on the ground with the kids, Groves rigidly stood his ground. Finally Andrews openly confronted him, with his by now almost comical defensiveness. Removing his kaftan, he urged Groves to follow his example, pointing out that a blue policeman's shirt was a cloak of authority that was no longer needed. Groves refused to comply, and when Andrews started to wrestle bare-chested with some of the lads, Groves stormed out, never to return.

Now Andrews was left with the problem of organizing the liberated energies of the kids into some kind of social and moral order. He was still, after all, running a youth centre. Gradually the novelty of the sheer presence of this 'crazy hippy' began to wear off, and the 'common language' that they had seemingly discovered through spontaneous play began to dry up. As evening followed unstructured evening, Andrews and the hard core of his members grew farther apart. An atmosphere of diffuse anxiety prevailed. Fights and breakages increased. Andrews resorted more and more to asking the trouble-makers what it was that they wanted. 'This is your place now, it's up to you to decide what to do with it.' But the invitation to participate had become a plea to co-operate, and after one particularly disruptive evening, Andrews reluctantly decided that negotiations had to be shelved. A direct order to a group of unruly youths to leave the premises signified the end of the personal and a reversion to the more familiar – to the kids – positional rules of conduct. But once an initially strong framework had been abandoned in favour of a weak classification of roles, the sudden reversal of policy could only reinforce the tense ambiguities of the situation. The members had their own ways of defending themselves against structureless-ness. Andrews was badly beaten up, ending up in hospital.

The Steelyard and the Shore Street Youth Centre illustrate some of the unintended consequences of a certain kind of radical strategy which today opposes traditional methods in classroom and youth club. Often this opposition is presented in terms of different attitudes to the young; libertarian against authoritarian. But if the whole argument is just about psychological attributes of individuals, of their ideological stances, then you pay your money and take your choice. It is easy enough to show how progressives can be highly manipulative in their dealings with young people and how traditionalists can behave in open and human ways.

What is at stake here is the objective consequences for the youngsters themselves of these different strategies, and of the different institutional orders which these strategies embody. How far, for instance, does the Steelyard Free School inhibit or develop young people's capacities to shape their collective destiny in class society? The irony is that advocates of 'structure', 'discipline', and 'maintaining standards' (such as the authors of the *Black Paper*) have an approach which *is* integral to – and reinforces – certain repressive structures in traditional working-class culture. Hence their considerable support, so shocking to the progressives, among working-class parents. The progressives are concerned to liberate youngsters from precisely these constraints of the parent culture. But liberate them into what? A classless environment created in the classroom? A common subculture of the adventure playground? And while the traditionalists leave unimpaired the kids' ability to recognize their situation in class, systemic terms, of Us and Them, the progressives often succeed only in blurring the picture. They may open up new horizons and help discover hidden talents, but these in turn can become a source of dissonance in the kids' lives once they try to pursue them in the outside world. Creative aspirations – learning to use a film camera, taking part in dramatic improvisation – all too often turn out to be non-negotiable currencies in the labour market.

And if such budding talent does find recognition then usually it is a one-way ticket to the déclassé limboland reserved in our society for the working-class 'success'.

Before it is possible to say a plague on both your houses, and set about a different problematic, it is worth reconsidering the one major context of working-class life where these contradictions appear to be resolved – a context where youth and parent cultures seem to find common ground; where learning and play, and with that instrumental skill and moral value, and with that collective and individual aspiration, interlock and display something like a peaceful co-existence. That context is sport, and the reality belies the appearance.

The Sporting Life

Sport was supposed to distract youngsters from more harmful pursuits as well as providing a useful entrée for them into respectable local life. On the Monmouth and Denby estates the legacy of this nineteenth-century intervention could still be traced in the Shore Street gymnasium and in the Sunday soccer leagues, although the evil these institutions were combating was now not so much physical as spiritual deprivation. The Father of St Joseph's Catholic Church, for example, who ran no fewer than four competition soccer sides drafted from the two estates, was applying his revised brand of nineteenth-century muscular Christianity to what he saw as 'this TV-watching and do-as-you-please society'. The best answer to boredom, alienation and anxiety was to 'work it off'. At a brains trust in the Church Hall, called after a spate of telephone-box smashing on the estate, the Father confidently advised youngsters to take up squash as an antidote to their more atavistic impulses.

But it was in the schools, rather than in the clubs of the neighbourhood, that sport was most successfully institutionalized by adults, finding there a context of aspiration and achievement that Shore Street Youth Centre and St Joseph's Church couldn't hope to compete with. Club and church teams could never be truly 'élite' squads. (Many of those who played for club sides virtually chose themselves just because they tended to play in their school teams.) But the school games field was a far more serious and astringent testing ground, and the talented young footballer or athlete knew it. Jock at Shore Street and the Father at St Joseph's would constantly complain that the school had first call on all their best players. Often a clash of fixtures would make it impossible for the club to field a team at all.

The cheerful moralizing of Jock or the Father was hardly in the same league as the tight-lipped intensity with which some school coaches approached their players. As a school team was put through the latest training techniques a slightly hysterical, frenetic atmosphere would prevail. Before the Big Game, the would-be Don Revie would attempt to fill his charges with a precocity of expertise and expectation more suited to their professional heroes than to schoolboys. Consequently, fourteen-year-olds would be seen in school matches playing with the machine-like intensity of the England national squad, with scarcely a glimpse of the qualities of spontaneity or selfishness on the ball that one would expect from ones so young.

In the middle-class grammar and public schools, sport strongly parallels academic endeavour as twin paths to 'success'. Hence the notion of the 'all-rounder' who is good at games and work and is therefore a likely candidate for head boy. In one large, tough all-boys comprehensive near the Monmouth, however, academic achievement was not for the majority, and a place in the school soccer team was a much more realistic stepping-stone to success. For a few there was even the chance of an offer from one of the local professional clubs, whose scouts watched prospects from the age of eleven. For other boys, sporting achievement as submission to adult discipline became an index of loyalty to the school; so most prefects tended to be sportsmen. These robust lads could often be more assured than their teachers of gaining an admiring and subservient response from the other kids.

Few successful sportsmen belonged to the grammar school

category of 'all-rounder'. Instead, there was the brilliant footballer who was also a lawless villain – 'He's a great goalkeeper. Mind you he's been nicked more times than he's saved goals.' Such an individual excited among his coaches a mixture of both admiration and envy, and exemplified the pull to the extremes of success and failure open to boys of his background. A school George Best would also be the main recipient of that special emotional relationship between manager and 'my lads'. In return for constant badgering to try harder and do better, young soccer rebels would be guaranteed the support of 'the boss', who would defend him, and the rest of his squad, against all critics, particularly fellow-teachers.

Sport, and in particular soccer, provided a pathway to recognition and success at school; in the clubs and Sunday leagues, acceptance into an established, respectable side of local life. But there was another side to the picture.

Despite the sign NO BALL GAMES, every evening improvised games of football would be played out on the courtyards and bare patches of grass around the Monmouth and Denby. Kids of all ages, shapes and sizes would take part in these, often in platform heels, smart jackets or tight trousers. Rules, playing area, goals, team numbers were all negotiable. What was harder to negotiate was the cooperation of the tenants. The broken windows, noise and disturbance caused by these games were amongst the biggest source of complaints that the Tenants Association Committee was called upon to deal with. Invariably, such matches would end in heated confrontations with angry tenants and the police being called.

Such casual disruptive exertions of physical energy tended to be seen by school coaches and club men such as Jock as little more than self-generating rituals practised by the kids as they are supposed to have done since time immemorial. Part of the local scenery. Quite different from the mini-professional training, coaching and adult-controlled sporting discipline as practised in club and school soccer. As one coach put it: 'There's very little competitiveness, very little possessiveness, on or off the ball, when they play in the street. They just get pleasure from making the ball move from one to another in a certain way, or just mucking about or showing off. But without any real energy put into it. In the youth club there's a lot more real fire goes into it . . . mind you, if I left them in the gym by themselves, if I wasn't there to watch them, they'd play like that . . .' Indeed, exactly the same kids would play these two styles out.

It is clear from this that attitudes to sport amongst these youngsters cannot simply be subsumed under one particular label. It is a long way from the public school sporting code of the 1880s to Manchester United's Stretford End. Yet planners and administrators still tend to see the appeal of sport and the need for it as universal. According to the Sports Council: 'Youth in particular needs the challenge and adventure of sport. Sporting competition – or conflict, if you like – provides an outlet for the aggressiveness of the young and for their natural desire to excel.'

It was in this spirit that the Riverside Sports Centre was completed in late 1972, as a much-needed community amenity for North London and as a monument to the universality of sport. The local Council, however, would only guarantee support with running costs (the building costs came from a private trust) if the Riverside was demonstrated to be fulfilling a community need. But which community? In its opening months, the Riverside became a hotly contested space, particularly amongst the kids.

The sporting ideal of the Riverside was to find its chief resonance in the community in the network of statutory and voluntary youth and sports clubs. Some six thousand school and club children would be block-booked into the facility every week. School and club bookings, ironically, stimulated casual use amongst the youngsters. A school visit might be a first introduction, a chance to meet and fraternize with kids from other schools and adjoining neighbourhoods. For as well as sporting facilities (squash courts, karate classes, cricket nets, badminton courts, etc.), the Riverside also boasted an ice rink and a plush coffee bar and refreshment area. The Centre was brand new and smart, and the ice rink a popular leisure as opposed to sporting facility. It was not long before some eight thousand children were attending weekly, to go ice-skating, sit in the coffe bar, chat each other up. Not a central part of the sporting objective of the Centre.

As different groups of kids arrived to stake their claim to this new territory, the Riverside became *the* key point on the local youth map. On the one hand there was supervised club use. On the other, casual use of the ice rink or coffee bar. On the one side, the mainstream of users in correct kit and carrying shower towels. On the other, dodging past the booking counter, gangs of lads in platform heels and tapered shirts. The Riverside became a battle arena where the conflicting aspects of a fragmented sporting ideology were acted out, whether through improving personal performance on the wall bars or in 'taking' a rival gang in the ice-rink toilets.

Over the first few months of its opening, the damage done to the building was estimated at a cost of twenty pounds a day, and the mainstream of users demanded protection. There were clearly two types of kid and two kinds of use to which the Centre was being put. As the head of the Centre put it to us:

Most youngsters are responsible and well behaved when they come here. But there are some kids who just want to disrupt for the sake of disruption . . . there were some I caught *spitting down from the balcony on to where the badminton coach was trying to coach some adults* . . .

Apart from the threat of a minority deliberately disregarding or resisting adult-dominated sporting disciplines, there was also the threat of that minority creating a subcultural climate of their own.

A couple of youths were in here who had a bit too much on drugs, and were causing quite a bit of disruption, and one of them was very sick and had to be got out of the Centre . . . It's nobody's fault but the pusher . . . It's an unfortunate situation, when you try to usher someone out who's on drugs; the person may think they're being got at and it may start a fight . . .

We don't want this to be a dead-end place. It can be great here. *We want to provide a sports facility, not a place pushers hang out and there's violence and vandalism.*

Within six months the Sports Centre went on to the offensive against youthful troublemakers. A squad of bouncers was recruited from amongst the young tough fraternity to take control. In addition, police regularly visited the Centre and frisked young visitors. Quite vicious incidents of fights and beatings were reported to us by kids from Monmouth and Denby who liked to visit the Centre. Meanwhile, a job on security at the Riverside became something of a status symbol amongst older graduates of the local fighting crews. Ironically, the mainstream of sporting users and club leaders, and school coaches, had to rely on the – in their eyes – most socially undesirable elements in their community to defend their recreational pursuits, while the 'unifying, universal appeal of sports' had actually sharpened existing or latent divisions and polarised mainstream and residual positions amongst the kids.

The provision of a new sports facility offered the opportunity to link the area's long-established tradition of disciplined sporting prowess with the needs of modern youth. But, initially at least, the Riverside policies seem to have created more bad feeling than good. It may therefore be worthwhile reviewing briefly the ideological premises of this kind of youth provision, the conditions of its success or failure. Strange to say, there is such a thing as a socialist policy towards sporting practice.

Mass physical education for all ages and both sexes, but particularly aimed at youth, and organized by either the State or the Party apparatus, is perhaps the one common denominator in the cultural policies of centralized collectivized régimes. In either case, Left or Right, this represents at once a progressive and reactionary movement as compared with the social organization of sport under capitalism: progressive in so far as the collective ideal takes the place of the Ideal Self as the support for mastery over techniques of bodily control; reactionary in that this collective ideal is appropriated to the State or the Party, where it resurrects the modalities of the Ideal Self personified in the leadership. Nevertheless this at least shows the importance of sporting practice for a humanistic socialism, that it offers one means of undermining the narcissistic cult of the body image which characterizes physical culture in capitalist society, and

131

which exerts such a perverse and regressive effect on adolescence.

In fact the continuities between capitalist and collectivist sporting régimes are as instructive as their differences. For both rest on the philosophy of the nineteenth-century rational recreation movement, with its notions that leisure must be earned by hard work, that it must be used as a means of moral self-improvement, and that it must be made as much like hard work as possible. So sport is taught and practised as discipline, approximated to work discipline, and in this way the gentleman ideal or the party ideal is inculcated in youth. In the process the play element in sport, its subversive aspect as a component of popular culture is systematically suppressed. Yet it is just this aspect which is important for a humanistic socialism, and which must be stressed in any libertarian approach to recreation provision. A principled approach to the physical education of adolescents is thus possible, though very rarely practised.

What is entailed is an approach which supports the play element against the discipline element, while emphasizing that sport is a collective way of keeping fit, not a support for the more narcissistic instances of youth culture. In the case of football, for example, this presumably means encouraging the spontaneous qualities of street kickabout, while at the same time discouraging the uses of the game purely as a means of individual exhibitionism; encouraging an appreciation of the tactics of self-expression over sheer spectacularism, and an understanding of the social history of the game, as opposed to the superstar qualities of individual players.

But the real importance of football for the kids comes from its existence as a mass spectator sport. On the terraces the association between football and violence and lawlessness remains pre-eminent.

Football, Football

A few miles from the Monmouth estate stands Highbury Stadium, gaunt, grey, monolithic, amid the run-down Coronation Streets of this part of North London. Formed in the 1880s by workers from the Woolwich Arsenal, Arsenal Football Club emerged in the thirties as the most famous soccer institution in the world, with weekly attendances averaging some fifty thousand. Despite attempts at modernization, the stadium itself, with its huge arcs of austere concrete terracing, still bears the marks of those times, when working men bore the brunt of the economic depression, and there were few pleasurable pastimes to choose from on wintry Saturday afternoons

In the inter-war years, the traditional assumptions amongst players and spectators about the nature of community – the affinities and emnities of 'place' – were played out on this pitch and passed on to succeeding generations. Here, as in many similar conurbations, supporters could feel part of the 'collective membership' of the club. Some even expressed a proprietorial interest. It was considered normal, for example, for the club to look at a promising young player recommended by one of the fans. But as we have mentioned before, after the war large-scale redevelopments led to the mass deportation of families and the breakdown of links between the associations of workplace and neighbourhood. In addition soccer now had to compete with television and a whole range of other leisure options which higher wage packets had for the first time put within the reach of working people.

There was a temporary 'soccer boom' in the forties, but by the middle fifties regular support for the 'Gunners' had started to decline, with some attendances at less than half pre-war levels. The team itself was playing poorly, and they no longer attracted floating supporters, unlike their close neighbours, Tottenham.

The bulk of Arsenal's drop in attendance occurred amongst the wartime generation of middle-aged working men, and their departure opened up a space for the kids on the terraces. A

133

prominent figure amongst the Islington mod gangs of the early sixties has recalled how teenagers no longer watched the game under the direct tutelage of their fathers and uncles.

We used to go up Arsenal together sometimes . . . It was terrible, mainly old men and little kids. The play was boring. We used to go sometimes and have a laugh among ourselves . . . There was no 'end' for the youth then, nothing like that.

This is one example of the mood of disaffiliation amongst local youth from the kind of spectator involvements delineated in the old soccer culture. Mod gangs, with their exclusively teenage affinities and enmities, cut across or ignored traditional adult boundaries. Watching football hardly compared with aspirations captured by the 'youth spectacle'. Not that mods stayed away from football *en masse*, or that many were not loyal fans. But the mods never seized on the football terrace for their public stage, as the skinheads were later to do.

It was against the background of such changes in youthful attitudes that a new soccer scene was to emerge. And here, other, material factors came into play.

The Kop

Youth 'ends' at football grounds did not spring up overnight. Before the war the bulk of the fanatical, sectarian supporters who stood together on the Liverpool Kop, or who massed behind the goals at Ibrox, Glasgow, tended to be mainly unemployed young workers. Football has long been a way out for juvenile unemployed, as well as older men, from the material oppression of their everyday lives.

On Merseyside, strong feuding traditions have long existed between the two main teams, Liverpool (Protestant) and Everton (Catholic), reflecting the antagonism between the parent cultures. In the middle sixties this was carried over into the patterns of recruitment of the respective 'ends'. The main body of the Kop still consisted of unemployed youth – unemployment in Liverpool being several times the national average – and they watched the game side by side with the older men. However, these youngsters did not still sing sectarian battle hymns; they brought with them into the ground the 'Mersey sound' and other traces of Beatles youth culture (long hair, gear, etc.) for which their city had become famous.

Away match travellers with the successful Liverpool team of the sixties, together with their northern, Scots and Irish contemporaries who had migrated south in search of work, brought with them rejuvenated versions of the paraphernalia of sectarian conflict; for example, the popular graffito K O P (or whoever) R U L E S – O K', which originated amongst the Glasgow gangs of the thirties, as a sign of territorial prerogative.

In addition the Kop improvised riveting choreographies, the most famous being the mass, swaying rendering of the Mersey hit tune 'You'll Never Walk Alone'. Then there was the rhythmic chant of team and players names – Li-ver-pool, Tommy-Smith, etc.

With such a repertoire the Kop provided an important source of emulation for young fans of teams throughout the country.

Bringing It All Back Home

As the rest of the kids copied these sectarian examples and formed fiercely partisan 'ends' on soccer terraces up and down the country, they also carried with them into the grounds their own tensions, created by the post-war changes in their own neighbourhoods. If unemployment had helped to power the Liverpool Kop, it was housing, the combined effect of thirty years of large- and small-scale urban redevelopment, that was to contribute to the changes on the terraces at Arsenal.

After the war many familes from Highbury and Islington went to settle in the suburbs and overspills – Uxbridge, Elstree, Borehamwood – which had sprung up on the fringes of the metropolis. Others moved to the new towns – Harlow, Stevenage, Welwyn Garden City – as well as expanding old towns such as Swindon. By the middle sixties the first generations of ex-urban youth had started to negotiate the shortage of public amenities – dance halls, cinemas, sports stadia – that seemed to have been planned in to these new environments. Above all, people complained of a lack of any definable central meeting places. All too often it was for the youth a story of nowhere to go and nothing to do.

Attempts to create some local 'life' often took a deviant course – drugs, gang clashes – and brought young people into conflict with authority. A minority got the message and preferred instead the migrant solution – from hanging out on Piccadilly Circus to casual work in the South Coast seaside resorts or even abroad. Others tried to maintain links with the old neighbourhoods of their childhood.

One of the strongest ways of doing this was through football. The game had changed considerably in the sixties. It was given spectacular treatment in the media following the excitement over England's World Cup victory in 1966. At the same time, following their successful fight for increased maximum wages, the image of professional footballers had become more glamorized, commercial. Gone were the pre-war days when footballers were humble club servants, hair neatly parted in the middle. Young star players like George Best, Rodney Marsh, and Charlie George looked and behaved more like pop singers. They were youth cultural as well as sporting heroes. The Arsenal terraces provided a natural focal point in the old locality for exiled teenagers, and it was the same in many other places.

In the 1966-7 season, on the popular North Bank terrace behind one of the goals, the Arsenal 'youth end' was born – suburban and provincial groups, and loose alliances of local crews, as this fan explains:

It's not just one mob – the North Bank. You've got the Essex Road. Now they'll wait outside one gate (for the rivals) and then, say, the Chapel Street mob, or the Packington, they'll come together or it'll be agreed like – waiting outside the other exits. We used to get the cunts

136

one way or another. We always used to have two or three really strong crews in there. And it was the same with the others. We used to have loads of different crews up Arsenal.

In fact people drawn from the immediate neighbourhood would sometimes account for little more than half of the combined strength of the 'end'. As we have said, much of Arsenal's support lies scattered around the suburbs; while a certain proportion comes from outside London altogether. And the pattern of location and age recruitment to the North Bank tends to directly reflect post-war patterns of resettlement. For instance, Watford has long been a traditional migrant exit route for local families looking to better themselves. And so 'the Watford' formed a small, tight-knit enclave amongst the shifting coalitions of local, ex-urban, and provincial groupings.

This overall pattern to recruitment has been accidentally highlighted by the actual physical layout of the North Bank terrace. It happens that the top section of the stand is divided by a corridor. Below it stands the locals, the Highbury, the Essex Road, the Packington, as well as the other 'London Boys', the Burnt Oak, the Hackney, even a few non-conformists from the East End, where West Ham United hold sway. Above the corridor, at the back of the terrace, often pressed right up against the corrugated iron awnings from where it is possible to see only about two thirds of the field, are gathered the ex-urbans and provincials; from Borehamwood to Swindon, from Basildon and Kidderminster to Uxbridge and Elstree. It's as if, for these youngsters, the space they share on the North Bank is a way of magically retrieving the sense of group solidarity and identification that once went along with living in a traditional working-class neighbourhood.

Apart from local gangs, ex-urban and provincial groups, small bands of youngsters are recruited to the 'end' through the same informal networks as put the word around about a good pub or disco. A fifteen-year-old school-leaver: 'I knew a geezer from school . . . a really hard kid. He goes, "Oh, you wanna come down the North Bank," so we went down there.' A lively scene

137

is promised, filled with the challenge of new faces, including girls, many of them unattached.

> There was all the scrubbers down there. All the girls wanted to pick up a bloke down there. Some would have a bang up against the metal at the back, by the corrugated iron. The North Bank's like a fuckin' brothel.

Yet girls are not just sexual appendages. This young fan's story confirmed our impression that what has traditionally been a male preserve has been to some extent opened up.

> There was this fuckin' great big girl, Linda. She must be six feet. She wears a pair of Doctor Martins. This geezer who was pissed tried to grab her. She gave him a right hard punch . . .

A cautionary tale!

The boys not only dominate whole sections of terracing, excluding the older soccer citizenry from the rights and obligations of this special 'freedom of the ground', they also open this freedom up to groups which had previously been only second-class soccer citizens – girls, and children, who form their own 'little ends' in many grounds.

Around these spectacular match day activities a whole underlife grew up, with everyday links in school playgrounds, factories, pubs, cafés, and discotheques. What is constantly being negotiated is the delicate system of territorial alliances that make up the 'end' (not to mention 'team ups' between rival 'ends'). You belong to the North Bank, the Shed, the Loft or wherever in so far as you demonstrate that the 'end' belongs to you and not to a rival group. Hence all the violent rituals of territory: taking the rival 'end', holding the home 'end', going up against rival supporters inside and outside the ground. Often a convincing victory by the home team on the field would provide proof enough of collective ownership, but as one fan put it, 'If they (the players) don't do it, we will.'

Sign of the Skinhead

As we suggested earlier, southern 'ends' like the North Bank adopted the mood of fierce, unswerving loyalty traditionally associated with soccer in the tough cities of Glasgow or Liverpool. At the same time, they also discovered their own models amongst the new generation of players: George Graham, a tough, crop-haired Scot; Charlie George, a local lad. These gifted players often gave the impression of flaunting the rules *and* getting away with it, thus contributing to their 'deviant superstar' status. What made Charlie George especially a hypnotic model for the 'end' was the air of street challenge about him, the 'look that spells bovver' – although not a word has been spoken or a blow struck – for some close marking defender; a look that suggested that if he wasn't equally at home sorting them out on the field he would be up there doing his share on the North Bank.

It was aggro, the sign of the skinhead, which became inextricably identified with the football 'end'. On TV and in the newspapers the label skinhead and soccer hooligan were virtually synonymous. Yet the skinheads neither created nor were created by the 'end'. What it gave them was a visible stage, a public platform – and what they gave back to the 'end' was a sense of itself, a common life-style. The skinhead phenomenon rallied the mass of young supporters on the terraces, and brought more kids in.

Contemporary followers of the Gunners, like Black Horse disco member Phil MacIlroy have made out of this a whole 'myth of origins' of the 'end'.

I dunno really what started it. The skinheads. Trying to chase the others out, I suppose . . . It just happened. One week you just saw the football like little goody boys. The next week it was a good kickin'. I dunno how it started. Skinheads got hold of it. I suppose someone nicked another kid's scarf and it went from there.

But being a skinhead soccer supporter did not necessarily mean that you had a criminal record outside the ground, or were a school failure. For example, Sean, a self-employed plumber who

139

lives and works near the Monmouth, recalled how in his skinhead days, 'when we first went down the North Bank [1967], some of us up there must have been twenty, twenty-three . . . we went down to cheer the lads, *watch the football and for a spot of aggro*'. One foot in the soccer culture of his elders, one foot sporting a bright red bovver boot. The latter he saw as a transitory thing, the odd conviction for causing an affray 'a part of growing up. It was silly, really, when you look back on it.' Sean continues to watch football, however. In his middle twenties and married, he follows the team from the anonymous fringes of the North Bank terrace, which encircle the hard core of the 'end'. Nowadays, he is extremely critical of 'young troublemakers who just go for the aggro', and in common with the majority of mainstream supporters he suggests bringing the birch back to deal with them.

Sean could also recall 'hard nuts up the end', for whom being a skinhead was not just a passing phase but virtually a permanent career structure; he also remembers the kind of leadership which presided over this youthful defence of territory.

When I first went down there you used to have leaders. A geezer called Johnny Briggs. And another geezer, fuckin' skinhead from the Packington, Leggo. They were like the hard nuts. He [Briggs] used to have a white butcher's coat with ARSENAL written all over it.

According to Sean and others, Johnny Briggs was the founder of the North Bank Highbury, the man who organized all the different groups together – a tough job! – but under him the North Bank was not 'taken' for four years – until the visit of Manchester United in 1972. During this period, the North Bank rose to become the loudest and most numerous group in London.

Thought to have been born on the North Bank, Briggs is described these days as being 8 feet tall and weighing 20 stone. Those closer to the happy event, however, have him a modest 6 feet 2 inches and 14 stone. Little is known about what he did for a living, though it was thought he had communications with the Big Highbury, a branch of the local villain fraternity. That he actually existed is certain, though; several times, turnstile operators were issued with his description, to keep him out.

On match days, Briggs and his lieutenants gathered in the Long Bar of the Gunner public house opposite the ground to lay field plans and assemble recruits. In particular, the armoury would be compared and passed around – from meat cleavers and sharpened combs to knuckle-dusters studded with broken razor blades. In contrast to Leggo, the 'fuckin' skinhead geezer from the Packington' mentioned by Sean, Briggs held no posts in the hierarchies of localized skinhead networks but instead preferred a derived status at a distance here. Besides, he was too old to run with the kids on the street. In all these respects, Briggs was an archetypal King of the Kop. In some ways, these early 'end' leaders were criminal versions of respectable traditional supporters, for both types try to pass on to the younger generation everything they think is important about the game. But Briggs's lessons to the four hundred odd adolescents around him were regressive-vicious displays of applied aggro. This message was passed on to excited little enders.

There are other elements, apart from the likes of Briggs and 'aggro merchants' like Leggo, which played a vital part in preserving the social cohesion and informal hierarchies of the 'end'. For example, the innovators of chants – the 'brains crew', and the 'wits' who took over much of the traditional functions of the classic cockney soccer-crowd wit. A player falls to the ground. A lone voice urges, 'Get some kip now, lad. You'll be back on the building site tomorrow morning.' A histrionic striker, missing an open goal, tears his hair. Voice: 'Don't panic, Stanley. Revert to Plan B.' During the double winning season of 1971, the collective voice of the North Bank showed itself to be as witty and original as any of its traditional predecessors. 'We're forever throwing bottles' sung to the tune of 'We're forever blowing bubbles' was reputed to have started here, as did the habit of a mass knees up (Muvver Brown) after a goal.

Football Crazy

The 'end' might have disrupted the surface pattern of crowd behaviour, but the continuities of the old soccer culture run far deeper. For example, Kevin.

Kevin, the nineteen-year-old barman of the Cross Keys, was a lifelong Arsenal supporter. He saw his first game at the age of six, supported on the shoulders of his father and uncle. In the years to follow he was to learn a lot from them about the club and its history. Alex James, Tommy Lawton, Joe Mercer, these were Arsenal's legendary players of the thirties and forties, whose exploits were matters of national as well as of local pride – 'ours were the best players in the world'.

Collecting autographs and cigarette cards, following the League tables, memorizing the results in the sports section of the newspaper, Kevin willingly applied himself to the art of partisanship and its accumulated folk wisdoms. He had less time for more academic pursuits. 'At school I played football three times a week, watched it once a week, talked about it all the time.' On leaving school Kevin followed in the footsteps of his father and grandfather and joined the Arsenal Supporters Club, a fraternity of youngsters like Kevin and more senior members, many of whom volunteered their services as crowd marshals. Supporters Club benefits included discos and socials, and chances to meet the players. The secretary could press for better ground facilities or even apply pressure to have unpopular players or managers removed. But the Supporters Club's main function consisted in organizing travel to matches away from home, including chartering flights and arranging accommodation for fixtures abroad. Supporters Club members had as little control over the directorial hierarchy of the club itself as anybody else who passed through the turnstiles. Kevin's main complaint, however, was that work obligations sometimes forced him to miss a game. Although this did not happen often, he was considering changing his job because of it.

Kevin's fiancée, although no fan herself, tolerated this passion for football, and even managed to put up with Kevin's severe post-match depressions when Arsenal's fortunes declined. Lately she had taken to accompanying him to some matches, 'to keep him out of trouble'. Although both were taught to see football as a male preserve, there was a place for steady girlfriends. Kitted out in red-and-white home-knitted scarves, the couple stood on the North Bank together with the rest of the younger Supporters Club members, immediately below the 'London Boys' and the 'scrubbers'. While watching a match Kevin kept up a running commentary, a kind of inside/outside broadcast on the game. Drawing from his wide knowledge and information, he continually scanned the game for its magic moments.

You go to watch the football, for ninety minutes. You go to watch it, for your team . . . you've got your idols . . . the players you look up to. You think he's terrific, you know. As soon as Chas gets hold of the ball you think, what's he gonna do now?

Although mostly biased towards his own team, Kevin could also be privately critical.

You watch a game, you want your team to win. But if you notice, you're picking out points. You're thinking to yourself, now that shouldn't be there. There's too much tactics. It's all planned, like a computer. You stand there, you say, gawd what's this, they're giving the ball away! You talk about it, you say, that player's just rubbish, you know.

Kevin's deep appreciation of the technicalities of the game stemmed partly from the fact that he also played it. But also the distinctive linguistic and cognitive styles at work here are very much the same as those used by his elders. Football talk, like trade talk, is the major way a working-class stock of knowledge is passed on and added to. In Kevin's commentaries a whole *mood* of appreciation and involvement is carried over from the family discourse as well. Not that Kevin was a prematurely middle-aged exception on the North Bank. Just the reverse. He avoided the older fans, preferring to transmit his commentaries on the game through the rough media of his peers.

Configurations of Youth

I wouldn't shout out. It sounds like the fucking old men. They shout out. Cross the ball! Cross the ball! Or Come on Arsenal! But in me mates, in there, in a group, you go, he fucking should have crossed that there, or that ball should have been cut out and all this. *But you just say it to your mates.* You see the old blokes, they shout out. They stand there with walking sticks. They shout out, you're rubbish and all this . . . *But with us you keep it between your mates.*

Here we can see the real change that has taken place on the terraces. Styles of spectatorship are no longer regulated and transmitted through the parent culture but directly through the peer group.

However, not all of Kevin's peers had time for the subtleties of his analyses. For many, football just meant Action, dramatic goalmouth incident, the way it's presented in the media – and it meant aggro with rival fans. Since they had little time for the football, Kevin had little time for them.

Some of the kids there . . . they came 'cos they'd heard about the North Bank, aggro and all this. They're demented. They don't know nothing about the game. They can't play football. They might know how to kick a ball, but that's it. They don't even know the names of our players. They're not bothered.

In the light of this condemnation, it is ironic that when he was younger Kevin had been thrown out of the ground several times – for fighting. Yet he had no reputation as a fighter, and was well behaved in civilian life. Kevin simply had a split perception about North Bank aggro.

You're watching a game as well, but if there's a bit of needle (among the fans) you go down there. You can't have a game for ninety minutes where it's action all the time. It gets boring, drab in places. Maybe it's only four or five minutes at a time. Maybe it's a quarter of an hour. But in places it gets boring.

Even if lads like Kevin had wanted to keep out of trouble it would have proved difficult after the crowd had been upset over a bad refereeing decision, or the excitement had spilled over during a big match.

When Chelsea come down . . . in the F.A. Cup . . . we was all packed tight, right the way across . . . There was thousands of the bastards . . . The tension, it was like a matchstick clicking.

In this type of atmosphere the few, older 'hard cases' would sense their moment to strike home, in the indiscriminate rampage that would follow, only they would not feel panic and fear, and Kevin would be swept along in the thick with them, whereas he would normally keep his distance from such people. The police, hired by the club to keep order, would intervene, and, as far as they are concerned, 'they all wear the same scarves'. A friend of Kevin's who never went up to the North Bank, and disliked the violence, had his arm broken by a policeman trying to calm unruly fans. Compared with Johnny Briggs and the other aggro merchants whose activities hit the headlines, young supporters like Kevin have only bit parts in the North Bank. Yet Kevin is one of many thousands of youngsters throughout the country whose lives are completely centred around football.

To me, football is everything to me . . . I don't mean that I would kill myself for it, but football is something that, you just get to love it, you know, you get so involved in it you can't go without it. When I was thirteen I broke my left ankle, hospital said don't play football . . . I was out playing football about three nights after, that's the sort of thing it is. Now I play about twice, three times a week, support Arsenal every time I can. My dad's the same. When you get it in the family it sort of comes down to you, you know.

Football means pleasure, as opposed to the pain of most people's working lives. It means sacrifice, as opposed to the impositions of daily routine. It means commitment, as opposed to detachment and cynicism about so many other things. There's a strong contrast between Kevin's apparent poverty of intellectual performance at school and his knowledge and fluency when it comes to talking about football. This parallels the contrast between the sedentariness of many of these kids' weekday lives, their reluctance to leave their immediate neighbourhoods, their frankly surreal mental maps of the rest of the city on the one hand and the high degree of organization some display in handling the logistics of free and cheap travel to away games throughout the length and breadth of the country, on the other. Does all this mean that football has a crucial therapeutic function? In the words of Phil MacIlroy:

You could have a terrible week, a bust-up with your girl, row with the old man, lose your job, everything could have gone wrong . . . But when you go down there, on the terraces, you're shouting along with the rest . . . your worries fall away, you're top of the world.

This is the classic working-class therapy of getting by, making the best of a bad job. It has nothing to do with the painful graft of working through the real problems of life. But football will continue to generate vital sustaining fantasies for adolescents who will otherwise become 'disturbed', until the basis exists for real material change in their lives.

Champions

In 1971 Arsenal did the double, winning both League and Cup competitions in the same season. It was grudgingly recognized by the club's directors that the strength and consistency of North Bank support both at home and away had been a major factor contributing towards the team's success. And while Arsenal headed the League, on the youth soccer grapevines of London word quickly spread that with a hard core of several thousand amidst a terrace capacity of eighteen thousand, for this season at least the North Bank Ruled.

Yet even at its height there were signs of the 'end's' inherent instability, indications of its imminent decline. This is not surprising when we remember that we are talking about a cosmopolitan and volatile assembly of adolescents who at the same time hold a collection of diverse attitudes to the game. The 'youth end' may appear a straightforward phenomenon from the outside, but its central dynamics are extremely complicated. Something of the inherent complexity of the 'end' may be gathered from the following piece of peer group analytics from a seventeen-year-old Arsenal supporter.

People think to themselves, I live near Arsenal's ground, I'm gonna support Arsenal. The majority of people support their team 'cos it's the easiest to get to. Ten pence bus ride. Others support a team 'cos they like the team. Maybe the style of football they play, maybe some of the players they got there . . . They might live near Arsenal but they really appreciate West Ham so they go there. With Man United, they're the team kids in London, the London Reds, think their supporters are the hardest. They wanna be part of them . . . It's got nothing to do with the football Man United play, they admire the Stretford End more than the team . . . If you thought you had to support the best team everybody would be supporting Liverpool, Leeds, the top teams. There wouldn't be no other supporters in the country . . . Success isn't the most important thing, it's got most to do with where you live, which team you support, or where you used to live before you got moved out . . . you go back there, support your old team . . . *So you've got your different types of supporters. But when they're at the game they're all supporting the same team, they're supporting Arsenal. But they're supporting Arsenal for different reasons.**

The decline in numbers and influence of the skinheads in the early seventies deprived the 'end' of the unifying symbolism under which all those different reasons for being Arsenal supporters referred to above had been subsumed. But at the same time the passing of the skins also meant the passing of all but the most residual of mass neighbourhood gangs of (white) youth in Highbury and Islington. The football mob became the only viable replacement to the point where it actively started to intervene in the geopolitics of London youth. More and more 'end' to 'end' warfares were carried over into the close season. In June 1974, for

---

*This is the best account of the sociology of the football 'end' we have come across, and is a good example of what we mean by class analytics. The lad's own experience, and those of his peers, filter through in the account, to make his understanding of a complex phenomenon concrete, and above all there is the need to communicate and make sense *to others*. The speaker was a trainee messenger boy with the GPO. He went on to blame violence at football on to 'the blacks', incidentally. How to develop the powers of class analytics here?

example, Chelsea boys fought Arsenal in a prearranged battle in the West End of London.

The biggest change in 'end' life in the seventies involved the passing of its original members – the class of sixty-eight; and not all of them 'graduated'.

The transition into the seats or the Supporters Club positions, like Kevin's, or into terrace anonymity, like Sean, was impossible for the hard-core skins like Leggo, or 'end' leaders like Johnny Briggs. Most of their social life depended on the existence of the 'end'. As the original 'end' began to disintegrate, as the bulk of its ageing membership graduated into the various adult positions, they became increasingly isolated. Johnny Briggs, banned from the ground, retreated to the Clock End for a time, and from there to retirement, some of his mates say prison, by the early seventies. As for Leggo, the transfer fee demanded by the social order for professional skinheads was a prolonged stay in borstal.

Gino, a seventeen-year-old from the Highbury Roundhouse, a loose-knit gang containing many white immigrant youth as well as victims of rehousing, points to the disappearance of 'end' hierarchies following the double winning season.

Nowadays [1973] you don't bother about it, having leaders. You're all in your little groups, and you form into a mass group. I know a lot of 'em as well as my own mates – in the Roundhouse. Some you don't know. You look at 'em, you can tell where they're from. You can suss out which lot's which.

Not surprisingly, the departure of an older youth hard core leads to a kind of regression of age roles. Our own surveys show that the average age of 'end' residents had dropped from 17–15 in 1968–72, to 15–13 over the next two years. And this was confirmed by those on the spot, like Gino.

The ends are getting younger. Not just our end, the others as well. There's nobody much older than seventeen around now [1973]. You see all the kids walkin' around in a big group, little hard nuts, with boots like, acting like they're older, thinkin' they're hard.

This younger generation, many of them graduates from the 'little end', show little sign of reproducing the hierarchical diversity of the original 'end' within themselves. They reproduce only its state of disintegration. Gino, at the top end of the age hierarchy, spoke contemptuously of 'little hard nuts, acting like they're older'. This is the essentially playful violence of school kids in a playground, but being taken out for real on rival supporters, while fantasies of dissociated violence replace the game itself as the main attraction.

The 'ends' may have got younger, less socially cohesive, but this does not necessarily mean that they were more violent. The North Bank, for example, with its 500 odd hard core, was relatively stable in the 1974 season. Hemmed in by rows of police officers, they were beginning to appear as traditional a feature of the ground as the colour of the players' shirts.

As elsewhere, the older unemployed, unskilled youth from whom the 'hard cases' are drawn had begun to congregate in less efficiently policed sections of the ground. For example, Nicos, a friend of Gino's – unemployed since he left school, and often in trouble with the law:

> You go down the Clock End now [1974]. Not the North Bank. You have a knuckle then. Don't matter who you're up against. You see a lot of the kids, there's gonna be a knuckle . . . there was a few of us, about six, up the front, running down there straight at 'em, ready for a knuckle. The North Bank was cheering us on . . . You don't care a monkeys, the other kids, just walk around with yer then, just to look tough.

And so the separate reputation of the Clock End is established, and recruits won over . . .

Older North Bank graduates have not departed entirely. On one occasion in the 1974–75 season, Arsenal were a goal down in an important match. The referee refused a penalty to the home side. A group of young men, mostly in their early twenties, spilled over from the stand seats on to the terrace to give the Clock End a helping hand.

We Hate Humans

The past few seasons have seen the rise of a non-territory-based, militaristic 'army' of young supporters – the Stretford End. This red-scarved mob of Manchester United followers are drawn not only from Manchester and its locality but from all over the country. They are mainly unskilled or unemployed and migrant young workers, social misfits, and plain soccer fanatics. Away match visits, where they cause the most trouble, are organized through the nationwide branches of the Supporters Club and more informal networks of young men in their late teens and early twenties, some of whom are as proud of the image they have foisted on to the rest of youth as being 'the best fighters in the land' as they are of following a famous team.

The North Bank Highbury was first confronted by this new kind of terrace organization in the spring of 1972. Manchester United were the visitors, and a thousand of their supporters marched from Kings Cross Station up the main road skirting the Monmouth estate to the stadium. On the way they broke windows, smashed up cars, threw rocks and swore at passers-by. Scattered groups of local youth shouted defiance – from a safe distance. At the end of the day the Stretford End had not only 'taken' the North Bank, but the whole of this part of north London.

The effect of visits like this was to reinforce United's support outside Manchester. Recruits from Arsenal territory included junior and senior tearaways from the disparate fighting crews of the neighbourhood. If you are out of work, a school failure, with little to do and nowhere to go, there is a great appeal in joining up in a supra-local soccer army with a national reputation.

We have seen how for the loose coalitions of the North Bank Highbury the football 'end' was a magical way of expressing collective ownership. You belong to the North Bank in so far as the North Bank belongs to you. But the North Bank is not owned by the kids, or their parents, or the organizations of their community, but by Denis Hill-Wood, Chairman of the Arsenal Board of Directors, who sits on the boards of thirty-two other companies. In the long run no one can 'magically' appropriate what in reality does not belong to them by virtue of their working-class place in society. The pathos and futility of fighting amongst rival groups of socially dispossessed youth is the best demonstration of the extent of the victory of those who really do hold the class power over them.

In this light the Stretford End heralds the growing nihilism of the youth soccer scene. The regular escalations of violence are only tenuously linked to the protocols of territory. Soccer itself is the pretext, rather than the structuring context of 'aggro'. The Stretford End chant, 'We Hate Humans!', is the best indication we can give of the present deranged mood of many of these youngsters.

Aggro Politics

What is the political significance, if any, of the soccer phenomenon? Here is something that commands the loyalties and mobilizes the aspirations of massive sections of working-class youth. Labour and trade union leaders, however, see in the youth soccer culture only a reaction, indeed a reactionary formation. But the football 'end' has been hailed by some members of the new Left as a manifestation of spontaneous collectivism behind which can be detected natural capacities for self-organization and leadership. Let us test these interpretations against a case in point.

The intervention of the Millwall 'end' at the big Vietnam Solidarity demonstration in central London, organized at the beginning of the 1968–69 soccer season, seemed on the face of it to provide ammunition for both points of view. The exuberant discipline of the Millwall crew, a phalanx of some two hundred skinheads in full chant, contrasted visibly with the students' individual attempts to improvise a similar choreography. But while petit bourgeois youth were affirming their commitment to revolutionary socialism – with chants of 'Ho, Ho, Ho Chi Minh!' – their proletarian counterparts were replying with 'Enoch, Enoch!' and 'Students, Students, ha, ha, ha!'

However, once the specifics of this confrontation are examined in greater depth it is not so easy to annex the position of the Millwall or any other 'end' to that of a youth vanguard, whether of the new Right or the new Left. Millwall is of course a dockland team. Uniquely amongst London clubs, its youth 'end' remained within the boundaries and traditions established by the parent soccer culture. Its operations were in fact supervised by a leader-ship group of dockers, men in their late twenties, and the kids were certainly politically influenced by them. This was a period of growing uncertainty in the dockland community. The first effects of containerization were being felt, and with them the threat to job security which dockers had for so long struggled to achieve. Equally dockland was beginning to suffer the effects of planning blight; the area was moving from near slum conditions to outright urban decay, while in some areas comprehensive re-development had made effective inroads into traditionally tight-knit communities. The large-scale influx of Asian immigrants into the East End made them an almost inevitable target for the accu-mulated resentments experienced by the indigenous working class at this time. The skins were not slow to act out the feelings of the parent culture in their 'Paki-bashing' phase. The dockers them-selves were to march to the House of Commons in support of Enoch Powell's immigration policy and his struggle with the Tory leadership.

All this does not mean that the Millwall's action at the Vietnam demonstration can be put down to political mimetism, a pure carbon copy of the attitudes or behaviour of their parents. The influence was formal rather than substantive; the context of their intervention, the function of their slogans, was profoundly different. The demonstration itself was no ordinary one. From the beginning it had been publicised, and not only by the media, as London's version of the 'events' of May 1968 in Paris. Here was a real political mimetism at work as the British student Left tried to emulate its peers on the left bank and lead the 'revolution' out of the campus and on to the streets. Yet it was not the spectre of revolution which stalked the streets around Grosvenor Square on that hot afternoon, but its spectacle. And it was as a spectacle that it attracted the skins' attention. Their intervention was essentially opportunistic, an attempt to go where the action was. They came down to Grosvenor Square in the same spirit, with the same purpose, as they went to an away match. They came to 'take' the rival crew, here represented by the students, and to capture the rival 'end', here the 'demonstration spectacle' itself. The slogans of socialism, the imagery of violent revolution, had all been confiscated by the opposition; in the Millwall skins' eyes all this had become the insignia of a petit bourgeois youth culture which that day had mobilized a hundred thousand on the march. The only signs of their class difference still available to them in this situation were those of their own strictly territorial identity as the Millwall, coupled with their subcultural presence as skins.

So there are no easy equations between the spontaneous – and therefore highly overdetermined – forms of the football 'end' and any received forms of political organization. This does not mean that the ultra-Right has not made attempts at entrism. The National Front has succeeded in getting its members elected to positions in supporters clubs and they have adapted football 'end' chants to carry their slogans on street demonstrations. Nevertheless the very complexity of the youth 'end', the unevenness of its developments, militates against such crude political manipulations.

We Gotta Get Out of This Place

The fact that they lived in an area with deeply rooted traditions of both in and out migration exerted a deep effect on local kids. Since the system of the putting out of kids as servants to other households, declined in the late eighteenth century, urban migration has been a major response for working youth to problems created by lack of domestic autonomy, unemployment, overcrowding and inelasticities in local housing and labour markets. And a way for them to continue to contribute to the family income, while not drawing on its resources. In addition, in certain historical circumstances migration has served to demarcate a period of 'youth' between leaving school and settling down. In both these respects it has provided an alternative to local youth cultures, but its function is the same – it leaves the problems intact for the next generation to face, while depositing its own layer of youth tradition as its special bequest to them.

We are talking here about what could be called 'drift' migration – a pattern of transience very much geared to seasonal fluctuation in demand for casual and unskilled youth labour in certain sectors of the economy. It is a pattern which all too often means periods of unemployment and a drift into petty crime.

The youth of the Monmouth estate knew all about the ins and outs of this kind of migration. They saw it going on around them every day, as penniless kids arrived at Kings Cross from Scotland, Ireland and the north-east. Many of their own parents had been through it, and they had heard their stories. They had no desire to repeat the experience. If they were going to make a move, it was going to be to better themselves in a very precise sense.

There were two paths open to them. The first was to join the armed forces. In fact the forces' recruiting campaigns very cleverly exploit the underlying motifs of both the kids' own subcultures and betterment migration: plenty of mates and girls, independence from home, excitement and travel; while more instrumentally, it offers the chance to learn a trade skill which they missed at school, and ensures they don't return to dead-end jobs when they go back to Civvy Street. But on the Monmouth, the role of the British Army in Ulster had made this option more than somewhat unpopular amongst many would-be young migrants. The other option was much more attractive: emigration abroad. And abroad was talked about exclusively, as tradition demanded, in terms of the white Commonwealth countries. Emigrating to Canada, Australia, New Zealand, the chance to play the wild colonial boy, was a routine topic of conversation amongst these lads. The girls too talked about the possibility, but in their mind's eye the key image was domestic – a better life for young married couples, a better start for the children.

It was strange to hear these young people, who, as we've said, rarely went out of the neighbourhood, talk eagerly of these far-off places, often displaying considerable knowledge about them. It wasn't just wild talk and dreams. Quite a few of them had relatives who had already emigrated to these countries. Their letters were filled with glowing accounts of the new life, and these were eagerly seized on as confirming the incentive to go. There was a pervasive feeling among many of the youth on the estate that Britain was finished; they wanted to go to a 'young' country, some place where young people were given a chance. The fact that this was a period of subcultural decline, the feeling that their generation had somehow missed out, undoubtedly contributed to this sense of disillusionment.

For many then, the desire to emigrate was based on a realistic appraisal of their life chances, or lack of them, in this country. The tragedy was that the more desperate an individual situation, the more desperately he or she wanted to get out, but the more difficult it was to leave.

For example: John Mitchell

John had been working as a rubber moulder in a local factory. He'd been there almost since he left school. He'd been getting a reasonable wage – £25 per week, including overtime bonus. And he needed to. His father was an invalid, his mother went out to work as a cleaner, which didn't bring in much, and there were two kids still at school. So the family relied on his contribution – £8 a week – to maintain a fair standard of living. John was also saving up to emigrate to Canada. His cousin was already there working on a farm, and had said that he'd help John with a place to live and finding a job. John had already saved £80 towards the fare – he reckoned he needed about the same again. It also seemed very practical. Especially as he was nearing his eighteenth birthday and was looking forward to getting adult wage rates. But his boss had other ideas. As the day neared, John complained that the foreman had started picking on him – having a go at him about his work, showing him up in front of the other lads, and other kinds of petty harassment. One day John blew up, told the foreman where he could stick his job and walked out. He quickly cooled down and next day went back to apologise and ask for his job back. Instead he got his cards.

John went to sign on. But, as he'd been fired, he didn't qualify for unemployment benefit. So, for the first time in his life, he went down the Social Security. He was shocked when they told him that as he was under eighteen and still living at home he was entitled to only £4.50 a week, and that for only four weeks.* This meant not only that his family's standard of living was cut by a quarter, but he couldn't keep up the hire-purchase payments on his moped, or pay the tax and insurance which, unfortunately, were due at this time.

He was determined not to give up the moped. Apart from anything else, it was the means of getting about to look for a new job. But then disaster struck. Coming home on the bike one night after a party, he was stopped by the police. And that meant charges of driving under the influence of alcohol, driving without tax and insurance and, because he argued back, assaulting a police officer. He was lucky. It was his first offence and he got off with a fifty pound fine and ten quid costs. Instead of asking for time to pay, he told the magistrate the truth about his savings, and so he was ordered to pay on the spot or risk imprisonment. Canada began to recede rapidly into the distance.

Then, to make matters worse, his cousin flew over for a short holiday. If John could get the air fare together, he could come straight back with him. As far as John or anyone else could see, this was the only way out for him. But what could he do – no money, no job and no transport. He was totally immobilized. And so in desperation he decided to 'do a job'. It was his bad luck

* No allowance is made for the fact or level of the young wage-earner's contribution to the family income. Instead, a 'lodger's allowance' is made. This, coupled with the punitive use of the four-week rule, is many kids' first experience of the benefits of living in a welfare state.

156

that in this particular department he had no experience and, he soon discovered, little aptitude. He decided to do a local tobacconist – he'd worked there on the paper round when he was younger and knew the takings were left in the till over the weekend. Inevitably he bungled it and was caught red-handed by the police.

In court his lawyer explained the full background to the offence, and made an impassioned plea for him to be let off so he could start a new life in Canada. The magistrate was unmoved. Commenting that he didn't think Mr Mitchell would be much of an asset to anyone else's country until he'd learnt to behave himself as a citizen of his own, he sentenced him to borstal training, thus effectively depriving him of any chance of ever emigrating anywhere.* Because he'd mentioned that he was hoping to work on his cousin's farm, the authorities thoughtfully sent him to an open borstal in the country. And that is as near as John Mitchell is ever likely now to get to achieving his dream.

He did his time. He was popular with the other borstal lads and earned a bit of a reputation as a tough nut. When he came out, he found that his old group of mates had dispersed, some had settled down, others had left the area, or drifted apart in other ways. His old girlfriend was now going with someone else. He was already embittered by his experience. Now, for the first time, he was lonely. He began to act hard and got into violent rows at home. He was so worried about this that he went to see his local doctor, who referred him to a clinic for disturbed adolescents. The clinic diagnosed a 'paranoid homosexual panic' . . .

Scottie

Scottie lived with his mum and dad in a flat in Cambria House on the Monmouth. Dad, a seaman from Hong Kong who had come to England as a kid, had a habit of walking out of home every few years. Scottie was very close to his mum. An only son, who

---

* Commonwealth countries do not admit people who have been imprisoned or found guilty of committing a serious criminal offence. Occasionally the rules are bent – it helps if you are a Member of Parliament.

could relieve her bitterness over her husband. A popular lad, quiet but sociable. And hard. In his late teens, dressed sharp. Good-looking. Popular with the girls. The final year at school had become increasingly irrelevant to his new career of disco habitué and 'bird-puller'. Left school. Got a job in a warehouse.

Problems at work. But his new career on the Scene grew by leaps and bounds. His seventeenth birthday saw a hectic gradua- tion into The West End rhythm and blues club scene, and a flirta- tion on the fringes of hippy flower-power. Got into drugs, pills, dex, hash. Flamboyant in dress, to put it mildly. Dressing up has always been a working-class thing, but the working-class London semi-hippy is something else again. Gold earrings, waist-length hair, leather pants, medallions, make-up the lot. And loads of girls. However, by nineteen, 'work hassles', and the deepening crisis at home, finally caught up and took their toll.

Scottie, the Golden Boy with a self-image of that description actively nurtured by his mum, who was now alone again, was now Scottie the Bad Son who was just like his dad and didn't want to be with his mother any more. He grew very depressed, especially at home. He went to the Out Patients at General Hospital. What's the matter with you, son? I dunno. Near to tears. Take these, one a day. Three if necessary. Come back if they don't work. With the loss of his job and in the throes of an emotional crisis, his career on the West End club scene came to an unhappy end. Scottie convalesced among his own people. Class convalescence, 'in dear old dirty Holloway', as he once put it. The milieu would sentimentally nurse his wounds. He took up with his old school mates again: two brothers, quiet, cautious lads, who were his best friends at school and were now working in the local butcher's. *They* had hardly been out of the borough in their lives. They supported Orient every week. They were well known to the mothers in the area – the butcher's boys. Conservative in dress, without being old-fashioned. 'It's not what you wear, the important thing is to be smart and clean.' The brothers welcomed Scottie home with wordless satisfaction, and they drank together every night in their local. This was Scottie's new routine. A quiet drink and a chat of an evening with his old mates. A colony of students from the polytechnic who lived near by were about the only other youthful patrons of this run-down old pub, and they and their numerous friends made their presence felt. The scene was set for Scottie's next sojourn into subcultural hinterland.

Scottie and the brothers started to get to know the students. The brothers shared the older regulars' latent hostility towards these invaders. There were frequent debates over attitudes to work, sex, drugs. Everyone enjoyed the arguments, but Scottie was less involved. His experiences had taken him into the company of far freakier people. Scottie grew particularly close to one of the students, Kathy, and slept with her. He thought about going to college himself – a vague fantasy with no lasting pull and little to back it up. Instead, he started to live the life of a student without actually being one. With Kathy, Scottie had time and encouragement to reflect on his life. Total reintegration with his old mates was impossible for him now. He moved out of his home and into a flat with Kathy and some of her friends. 'Not a hippy, not a freak scene, well what is it? They're educated but they defy authority'. Scottie absorbed the anger towards authority of these student militants; he even went along to a couple of demos. But he could never in a million years square their talk of the revolutionary potential of the working class with his own native grasp of the community.

Scottie's moving out of home deeply upset his mother. He was escaping again. As for the brothers, his best and most loyal mates – 'he's a great bloke, he is, whatever he does'. They were saddened, though, and bitter, as they sensed which way he was drifting, away from them and their local life. Scottie seemed strained in their company. There was little to talk about. OK they were his mates, but the students and Kathy have *interests*. Besides, the brothers 'will always be around when you need them.'

Scottie never quite fitted in among the students. His appearance grew progressively stranger. He was most happy not with his mates, not with his mum, not in his new job rejecting ice creams at Walls, but with the more disturbed elements of the student community. His relationship with Kathy grew strained. Back down to the Out Patients again. This was followed by a series of court appearances – breach of the peace, drunk and disorderly, obstructing the highway. Back home to an embittered mother in Cambria House. Sat in father's chair, 'looks a bit like his dad' – watching telly defiantly. Gradually back down to the local again. The barman pours him an unsmiling pint. And the students? Just one more transient group in an area with a long tradition of transience.

Collar

One evening Collar, a seventeen-year-old Monmouth lad, turned up at the bar of the Swan public house and asked if this was where the meeting of the North London branch of the Young Socialists was to take place as advertised. The landlord directed him upstairs.

Like most of his contemporaries on the Monmouth, Collar had never been near a political meeting in his life. Although working youth like himself, and groups of revolutionaries, met regularly in this pub, for all the contact they had with each other they might as well have been on different planets. But Collar had been having trouble at work – he was a trainee engineer with the GPO – and the heavy work-load and the pitiful wages annoyed and angered him. As for the union – 'they just don't seem to want to know.' He talked things over with some of his workmates, and one of them had shown him a newspaper with the headline in big red letters: YOUNG SOCIALISTS FIGHT FOR A BETTER DEAL FOR YOUNG WORKERS...

Collar's grandad had been a branch secretary in the musicians' union, so he had some idea from his family what 'socialism' was supposed to be about. He had expected that this meeting was part of some militant *activity* on those lines. As well as that, he had watched students in action on TV and that too seemed exciting – drugs, rock 'n' roll and liberated women, as well as battles with the police. Collar was in his own words 'just rarin' to go'.

As soon as he entered the meeting, his heart sank. A cold dingy room, piles of old newspapers, half a dozen people, a monotonous half-whispered discussion in a language he could barely understand. Collar was questioned closely by the comrades. Who was he? Where did he work? Did he know so-and-so? Was that who sent him? How did he find out about this meeting? Had he ever been to one before? Did he know anyone who was in the Young Communists or the International Marxist Group? Collar had never even heard of the latter organization, let alone been a member. After grilling the lad in this manner for some time, the meeting returned to its agenda and Collar was ignored. After an hour or so the gathering adjourned to the bar, and Collar was just about to wander off when someone handed him fifty copies of *Keep Left* and told him to sell as many as he could in his neighbourhood and in his place of work. See you next week!

Despite their fighting banner headlines, the image of militant workers sweeping all before them, the newspapers proved difficult to sell on the Monmouth. One evening Collar, dispirited, and irritated by the ribbing he was getting from his mates, dropped into the Swan for a drink. He was approached by a man with a beard who asked him if he was selling the newspapers he had with him. Collar told him he was trying to, but hadn't got very far. The man left without a word. Next week upstairs in the Swan, Collar found to his amazement that he was the only one who hadn't managed to 'sell' all his copies. He was then carpeted by an elderly comrade who had been informed that Collar had been drinking while carrying out revolutionary work.

Collar's initial hunger for some more relevant political activity was slowly being eroded by such petty rules and regulations. He soon learnt that selling newspapers was the only form of 'revolutionary action' permissible. The Party was aiming for a national daily sale and everyone's energies were being devoted to this, as it proved, illusory goal. Nevertheless, he made many new friends among the membership, and even went to Manchester for a National Youth Conference. He was impressed by the numbers of young working people like himself who attended. But the main resolution of the conference was disappointing – 'to redouble our sales'.

At no time did the leadership at the conference seem willing to listen to the younger rank and file; to take into account any criticism they might have – about the newspaper for example, most of which Collar found incomprehensible, written in some strange political code. After a year Collar finally got up the courage to deliver a long speech at a branch meeting. What has Trotsky got to do with today? He might have been a great bloke in his own time in Russia. What's he got to do with living in North London now? He was told that he was a reactionary and didn't understand Marx. Collar replied that as far as he was concerned this organization was just like a religious sect – if you didn't believe in the dogma you were out. 'You treat Marx like Christians treat the bible . . .'

Fortunately Collar had not got so deeply enmeshed in the Party organization that he had lost contact with his old mates and interests. He had been a probationary recruit, and he was never offered a Party card. It was from his roots in his own culture that he had made his criticism of the politics of this organization. A culture which this politics saw as the repository of 'spontaneism', 'reformism', 'adventurism', and other such evils which had to come under the hammer of the Revolutionary Party. If Collar had become more deeply involved it could only have meant gradual separation from his mates. Instead, the price he paid for staying with his mates was political disillusionment. Just as his mates had once said to him when he tried to recruit them, now it was Collar's turn to say, 'Politics? Leave it out! Socialism? Don't make me laugh . . .'

A comparison of these three stories, together with those of Billy Sheahan, Brian, and the Steelyard children described earlier, gives some idea of the kinds of variations in 'individual solutions' that, unfortunately, are possible. The reader may also observe some of these trajectories have a pattern about them. Sociologists, who study these things, often call them 'deviant career structures'. The picture this conjures up is of someone driving a car firmly in control of where it's going, even if it's off the straight and narrow. But it would probably be more accurate to call it a *careering* structure. The person may nominally be in the driving seat – after all it's his car – but in fact he is being given a whole set of contra-dictory instructions by a large number of back-seat drivers, some of whom are selves, some of whom are others. Although everyone may think that *they* are in control, the car itself is quite out of control, and often finishes by crashing into a dead-end turning (brick wall?).

It is only in so far as these young people remain anchored to their original nexus of class, community and culture that the conditions exist for them to organize collectively, and effectively (and that means politically) to tackle the recurrent problems which the individual solutions we've described do no more than perpetuate in a context of personal defiance and defeat. Therefore, strategies of intervention which dissociate sections of working-class youth from this nexus, whether they derive from the Alternative Culture or agencies of middle-class reform, have to be neutralized. Often the most effective source of resistance comes from a kid's own mates and family. But, as we saw in Scottie's story, this in itself, without more organized support, may not be enough. The problem of how best to reintegrate a highly marginalized youth back into association with his old mates cannot be solved overnight. But if any genuine strategy of re-placement is going to be possible, then first of all we have to have a way of deciding exactly where a particular individual is at – which is the determinant level in play, and often it is not the most visible one. And sometimes the process will have already gone too far, as in the case of Billy Sheahan, the truant.

Political educative intervention is also from 'the outside'. Its aim can only be to produce a shift in consciousness, at least as far as to make explicit the demands which are implicit in the kid's own culture. But it is important that this displacement is not reflected at other levels. This was the problem with Brian, leader of the Black Horse disco lobby. The situation was complicated by the fact that his family had recently moved from the area. But we were successful in ensuring that he didn't become socially isolated from his mates. Left groups, whose strategy of political education is modelled on that of religious conversion, would perhaps not be quite so careful. Indeed, Collar's story shows how

163

this kind of intervention can result in a marginality just as vicious as anything achieved by the ideological state apparatus. Collar had the sense and the resource to break back to his own people. But the price he paid was permanent political cynicism. The conclusion must be that, apart from occupational communities with a strong political culture which is transmitted from generation to generation through the family, such strategies are self-defeating, both for the organizations concerned and, far more importantly, for the vast majority of their young recruits.

Part three
Fighting the
New Nihilism

Backlash

In November 1976, over two hundred all white, mainly middle-aged people crowded into a hall near the Monmouth estate to voice their opposition to a proposed plan to extend Uhuru, the local black youth centre.* The meeting had been called by the Monmouth Tenants Committee, in conjunction with other big tenants' organizations in the vicinity, and proved to be the largest meeting of residents in the history of the estate.

Throughout the previous year, following the closing of the Black Horse disco there had been a number of violent incidents in the area surrounding Uhuru, the most serious involving break-ins and stabbings, and the anger of the tenants was increasingly directed against the drifting bands of unemployed, sometimes homeless, black youths who frequented Uhuru, who often stayed there overnight or dossed in nearby derries.

Noisiness, dirtiness, keeping late hours, the way one gang moved about the neighbourhood in an intimidating manner – these were just some of the complaints voiced against Uhuru members. Although, as one mother was to point out in the course of the meeting, 'our kids are no angels', in the eyes of most whites, blacks were to blame for every break-in, every smashed street light, every obscene wall graffito. The chairman of the Tenants Committee opened the meeting in Churchillian style 'We will fight to our last breath, to our last drop of blood, to stop these plans!!!' This was followed by a series of angry allegations from the floor. 'That place is the headquarters for black borstal kids from all over London . . .' 'They come here from Brixton and Ladbroke Grove . . .' 'It's a crime centre . . .' 'It's

* See page 115.

full of drugs . . .' 'It's a bloody brothel . . .' 'We're paying for it out of our rates and taxes . . .' And so on.

The director of Uhuru was attacked, in his absence, as a crafty manipulator, out to dupe the locals. Recently a fire had seriously damaged the centre. This was almost certainly the work of local white kids. But speaker after speaker claimed that the director himself had been behind it, gutting his own building so that it could be rebuilt with an extra floor. Even his offer to help in a campaign for a new pensioners' hall was denounced by several speakers as trickery.

A bluff local councillor, Grimes, addressed the meeting. He began by denying that he was a racialist: 'After all, in the midweek football league, the only thing that works in this borough, they've got dozens of black kids, and Greeks, and Turks, and there's no problem, as long as they behave themselves.' Grimes went on to suggest ways of putting pressure on Uhuru, and in particular 'the trendy left-wing councillors', with their 'agendas a foot thick', who supported it. 'You breathe on 'em, look over their shoulders, keep at 'em, and they bend. They can't take pressure.' According to Grimes, the Council 'wine and cheese set with their posh accents and big words' were the real culprits. 'These people fall over backwards to do anything for black people . . . They won't hear a word of criticism against them . . . I am sick and tired of these ''bleeding hearts'' . . . They give money to squatters, Bangladeshis, the lot . . .' As for community workers from the Meredith Neighbourhood Centre – 'long hair and plimsolls, they come here and think they can tell you how to live'.

This bitter tirade against petty bourgeois radicals, with its strong racist undertones, was received enthusiastically enough. But a speech from Sid Chambers, manager of the local Swan public house, proved to be the evening's star turn. Churchlike solemnity settled on the proceedings as Chambers told his story. One night three black youths had entered his pub clutching cans of beer and boxes of Kentucky fried chicken. He had refused to serve them, and had been prosecuted by the Race Relations Board for his pains. He was eventually taken to court and fined fifty pounds, but refused to pay. In fact, the Swan had long enjoyed a mixed clientele, without trouble, and the manager had some cause to refuse these lads. But whatever the truth of the matter, the majority of this audience preferred to see here yet another example of official backing for racial discrimination *against whites*, just like the plan to extend Uhuru . . .

The meeting ended in confusion. Plans for future action remained vague. It is precisely in the confusion surrounding such localized issues that the extreme right National Front flourishes, exploiting very real fears and frustrations of the white community to win an increasingly powerful base at the grass roots of working-class politics. The Front's message is that embattled inner-city neighbourhoods like the Monmouth and the Denby are victims of a conspiracy of interest between the whole economic and political establishment and 'the immigrant'. But although this often strikes a powerful chord, it is not from the ranks of predominantly Labour-voting council tenants at meetings such as this that active National Front cadres are recruited, but from amongst their children.

Punk Politics

In the Greater London Council elections of April 1977, a large section of white first-time voters in the Monmouth and Denby ward voted for the National Front. The relatively high turn-out of youngsters was typical of inner-city neighbourhoods with a high concentration of immigrants; National Front votes were piled up amongst what one survey described as 'the young, white, and ungifted',* in other words the kind of 'estate kids' that we have described in this book. In one area with a high proportion of immigrants near the Monmouth, a bus was organized to bring young Front supporters to the polls. This enthusiasm for the ballot box was complemented by voluntary canvassing. In the

* From a report by Harrop and Zimmerman, Department of Government, Essex University, June 1977.

weeks prior to the election, bands of kids could be seen purposefully stuffing leaflets into letter boxes, or daubing walls with National Front slogans and anti-immigrant graffiti.

Some kids even found themselves attending Front meetings, whereas months before they would never have dreamed of going to any kind of political meeting. Here are the impressions of one youth.

I expected flags outside, heavy geezers, things like that. But all it was – I went in there, sat down. There was this middle-aged bloke in a grey suit, and he had his daughter by the side of him, sucking her thumb. He was just talking. I expected to see hard blokes there, but it was nothing. It was more like a mothers' meeting. It wasn't like everything it's made out to be.

The tame meeting was disappointing to this lad because much of the appeal of the Front is summed up by their nick-names amongst the kids – 'the violent party' and 'the hatred party', and in their own slogan 'it's time to stand up to the immigrant'. The NF offers vital leadership and focus if, as many kids see it, the white gangs are ever going to 'win back' the streets from the blacks. In fact, in some kids' eyes the NF even has its own rival crew, 'the communists. They're the ones that say "we gotta get rid of the Front" and that.' But at NF meetings the quirky 'little man in a grey suit' image still prevails, and this is far less appealing to kids. Recently, however, the Front has learnt how to organize directly through some aspect of youth culture, for example by gaining influence in football supporters clubs and inculcating NF slogans through the medium of 'end' chants. At the same time NF cadres are successfully propagating the more sophisticated fascistic ideas. The Great Conspiracy between Big Business and the Immigrants, the Liberal Press and TV Censorship of the Race War, the role of the Reds in destroying a Once Great Country – more and more working youth are becoming familiar with these arguments, having read the necessary pamphlets, or discussed them directly with NF members in pubs, clubs and places of work.

Of course racism amongst youth did not just spring up overnight. For example, 'Paki-bashing' was the dark side of the skin-head phenomenon. Yet ironically it is with the decline of the skin-heads and youth subculture in general that the NF have bene-fited. (Of course they are greatly aided in this by the successive failure of Tories and Labour to 'solve' the worsening economic crisis, and the subsequent disillusionment of all sections of work-ing people with the political *status quo*.) The 1977 electoral swing to the NF took place against a backdrop of yet another convolu-tion of youth culture – the rise of punk rock and the Return of the Teds. The *déjà vu* nature of punk *v.* ted gang battles, the self-conscious paranoia of the music, and rejection of hippy peace and love, the return of the 'freak' underground press in the form of the punk fanzines, is the confused bric-à-brac of styles that results when youth subculture gives birth to its own! Meanwhile, the commercial entrepreneurs of youth fashion wait in the wings – punk, teds, rock 'n' roll, fanzines, all grist to the mill to be manu-factured into fresh scenarios for the TEEN SCENE.

Coffee and razor talk of teddy boy cafés . . . mods and rocker outings to the sea . . . fast rhythm and blues pilled nights in sixties discos . . . the long march of the skinheads from the North Banks of London to the Liverpool Kop. In Suffragette City young girls sopping with desire: 'I WANNA HOLD YOUR HAND!' as the Man with the Tan flings them from the stage, into the arms of Donny and Davy and the Bay City Rollers, and *Teen* and *Fab* and *Honey* . . . All aboard for the Six Five Special! And the ready steady merry-go-round of festivals, from the Isle of Wight to Itchycoo Park . . . Today a new generation and their housebound elders sit stranded before the telly, as the lights go up for always one more time on the golden days of rock'n'roll, where the faces may have changed but the songs go on for ever . . . And so to a hot summer night after the Hackney town hall dance 1977 . . . School's out and bands of diminutive Presleys, Deans and assorted young punks meet for the annual Hoxton *v.* Hackney derby, kitted out with bottles, knives, bricks – everything they need for the traditional East End rituals of territory. Four boys stabbed, one seriously. Over there the headlines of yesterday's conscience scream out, 'the Law is still beating up the wrong guy'.

This general mood of nihilistic, violent despair provides the per-fect setting against which an NF style party can flourish.

The 'cultural decadence' of the white kids, then, coupled with their social disorganization, and their structural isolation in the political geography of their own communities, makes them vulnerable to the kind of approaches which can apparently offer them precisely what they lack and which sets them at such a disadvantage in their relations with black youth. At the same time the inbuilt territorial chauvinism of these kids is being converted by the ideologies of right-wing populism into overt racism.

No Left Turn

It would be nice to conclude with a straightforward appeal for greater trade-union involvement with the concerns of working youth at the point of both production and reproduction. It would be nice to be able to counsel the radical alternatives movement in education and youth and community work to build stronger links with their local Labour movements. It would be nice to be able to solve the problem with an exhortation to unorganized youth to join trade unions, get active in the Labour Party or one of the Left sects, and become part of the traditional struggle for socialism. In the more frustrating moments of the Black Horse episode we often fell back on such suggestions. If only we'd had the backing of a strong and imaginative trades council or tenants movement. Or if we could have got behind them to their eternal rank and file. If only the role of 'socialist youth organizer' had been as readily identifiable to the kids as those of teacher, priest, or community worker.

In fact, if we erred in anything, it was in acting 'as if' these 'if only' conditions obtained. For the rest, we argued, our mistakes were largely forced on us by the nature of our intervention in a divided and fractious community where we were often made to act against our best socialist intentions.

Such comforting thoughts are beside the point. Easy equations for solving the dislocations within and between the formations of working-class youth and the grass roots of the Labour movement are not – if ever they were – on the agenda of possibilities.

Today in Britain the official class struggle has receded into the background of the lives of working youth as the struggle of old men. Although socialists are naturally anxious to create a viable working-class base – if only to restore Labour's hopes at elections – the organizations of the Left are dominated by the new petty bourgeoisie, students, academics, teachers, social workers – precisely that social stratum of whom the industrial working class, and especially its youth, have come to have such a profound distrust. The decline of working-class socialism has been part and parcel of the rise of petty bourgeois radicalism.

The position is aggravated by the fact that most Left organizations continue to fight the battles of the seventies with the tactics of the thirties, especially in their anti-fascist campaigns. In doing so what they draw on is a more or less sentimental image of a traditional working-class culture and community, whose institutions their very presence, if not their policies, have helped to marginalize. For example, middle-class socialists who buy up old houses and move into old inner-city neighbourhoods such as the one we have described, which effectively displaces the resident population, and then take over local Labour Party branches and trades councils, or obtain seats on the Council, often find that far from being regarded as 'friends of the people' they are, through no fault of their own, making class enemies and winning recruits for the Right.

In this context then, there is no hope at all that the petty bourgeois Left will win working-class youth for socialism.

Praise of Learning

Learn the simplest things. It's
never too late
if you're ready!
Learn to read and write, it's not enough

but do it! Don't get discouraged,
start! You must know everything.
You must control your own life.

Don't be afraid to ask!
Don't 'do as you're told',
work it out for yourself!
If you don't find out yourself,
you'll never know.
Figure it out.
It's your life.
Look around; take it all in,
ask: how did this get here?
You must be ready to take the lead.*

Educational Groups: A Modest Proposal

For progressive teachers and youth workers in the inner cities, it
should be clear that growing unemployment, racism, and
educational disadvantage amongst working youth are not being
ameliorated by laying on more and better disco nights at youth
clubs, allocating more and better table tennis bats, or servicing
more and better camping weekends. Against a background of a
deepening economic crisis and in a climate of overt racism, youth
workers cannot afford to distance themselves from the material
concerns of youth, or fall back into the role of latter-day pro-
viders of nineteenth-century models of 'rational recreation' for
the working classes.

What is needed are new strategies of social education which can
actually *reach* the kids, that steer equally between the rival shores
of socialist Sunday School and 'Top of the Pops', and between
sentimental middle-class therapeutics and the old-style authori-
tarianism.

* From *Praise of Learning* by Bertolt Brecht, freely adapted and abridged
by David Zane Mairowitz for the purposes of this book.

In our work at the Black Horse we ourselves tried to break out of the role of youth workers as a more or less superior form of child-minding. But we were still providing a youth *service* – running a disco club – *and we failed to break with the problematic of youth provision as such.*

We were confronted with a set of immediate demands, and the condition of our continued presence in the area was support for them. Unlike the mainstream youth service, we did not have to say to the local kids 'What you need is a disco'; they said to us 'What we want is a disco'. Though we did not hold to the populist maxim that The People is Always Right, we agreed that such demands, however 'false' or reformist, should in any case be supported, because through organizing around such issues, by winning small-scale victories, teenagers would gain a self-confident class awareness to the point where they would begin to make explicitly socialist demands in the strategic sectors of youth struggle – housing, education, local politics, and work.

Our tactic was to push the disco to the limits of its content as a demand, and in this we were undoubtedly successful. The campaign itself revealed capacities for leadership and struggle amongst local teenagers, precisely because it was a real exercise in their collective bargaining power as an interest group. When the disco opened, it was given a social direction so that the real demand it contained, and concealed, namely the demand for domestic autonomy and the need to transform the Black Horse into a fully fledged youth house, came into focus. But by virtue of its context, these aspirations could scarcely break out of the disco formula, but took the form of pleas for bigger and better versions of the same. More activities, more nights, more live bands and so on.

We were caught in a parallel bind. We had been committed to making the disco a success. That meant making the imaginary scenarios of Teenage Dream Time work as a social reality. But the more successful we were at this, the more we failed in our real objective – to break through their stranglehold on members' consciousness. It was only when the disco began to fail – as in the instance of one night when it actually ground to a halt – that we began to feel that we were successfully beginning to get to grips with the real issues. However, we could not afford to let the disco fail, for then we would have lost not only credibility with the tenants, but our constituency amongst the youth. To put it another way, the more successful the disco was in conventional terms, in getting large numbers of kids off the streets and into a Good Time, the more successfully it solved everyone's problems but their own. For example, the disco helped solve the local police problem of 'juvenile crime'. (We still have their letter of commendation to prove it!) And we solved the tenants' problem of estate vandalism. But as for the kids, we succeeded only in neutralizing their nuisance value in the neighbourhood, and hence their bargaining power, without putting anything more politically effective in its place.

Conversely, as soon as the kids began to take steps to go beyond the disco formula, then this began to create more problems of social control for adult agencies than it solved. The conclusion from this must be, not that the contradictions between parent and youth constituencies are essentially antagonistic, but that their interests cannot be resolved from the base-line of any model of youth and community provision.

So what we are suggesting, in place of the 'youth provision' formula, is the idea of youth work as social and political *education*, but not in the sense that this is usually practised by socialists. We are not talking about radical civics, or propaganda recruitment for this or that version of leftism; least of all, of a crash course of study Marxism for the masses. All these are traditional forms of counter-ideological inculcation, which working youth rightfully resent and resist as yet one more form of middle-class imposition on their lives. To adopt any of these approaches would be the best way to go about winning fresh recruits for the National Front. The kind of educational process we are suggesting is one which remains rooted in the peer group uses of language and literacy, as well as the oral traditions through which the residual forms of working-class knowledge are transmitted; but which also intervenes in them to develop their latent power as *class analytics*. It is a process, then, in which young people move from being simple narrators, to become the teachers, and finally the spokesmen of their peers.

What, concretely, characterizes such an educational process? What form would it take? Some of the answers to these questions may be derived from the following example of the successful practice of a socialist teacher.

In an outer working-class suburb of a big industrial city, there has been running for several years, almost entirely unknown to the authorities, a socialist educational group – or rather groups, because now there are three. Their founder and first teacher was a thirty-five-year-old laboratory technician, who has no paper qualifications but who, rather like the story-tellers of old, has the ability to explain complex phenomena clearly and excitingly to young people. He started by working as a volunteer in a halfway house for the rehabilitation of young offenders. Here he met John, a morose and unpredictable lad of sixteen who had been in almost constant trouble since he was twelve. He was classified as depressive, potentially violent, and non-verbal. The teacher took an interest in the boy, and one day John showed him some poems he had written. The teacher was impressed by the clarity and assurance of their language. He had got to know the boy's parents meanwhile, and he started to give the lad lessons in his home. The educational group had begun. He became known on the estate as 'the teacher' who worked with John. He spent many evenings explaining informally to local youth and their parents what he had to offer. He explained that he would teach reading, writing and the history of socialism, free, two evenings a week. There would be no exams, of course, but students would be expected eventually to leave and, he hoped, to start an educational group of their own. These ideas were greeted at first with a mixture of amusement and incredulity, but the teacher was generally liked, and his lack of pomposity and his sense of humour, coupled with his toughness, won him respect. His message was that 'young people had come to learn and learning does not come without hard work.'

Soon the group had eight members. Its life varied in its progress. For a while everything would go well, with maximum attendance and even some curious newcomers. Then, for no apparent reason, the teacher would turn up at his usual meeting-place and there would be nobody there. Not one. Or perhaps one. But whatever the sorry state of affairs the teacher would not conceal his anger from the kids, but confront them directly, expecting a straight answer. On such occasions parents might also be approached, and at all times they would get, whether they wanted it or not, a formal report on their children's progress and discussion of any problems. Parental responses varied from apathy, sympathetic interest to outright hostility. Through the local tenants association the teacher was given a small shed amongst the garages on the estate. Now the group had a permanent base, although it still met from time to time at members' homes. The teacher went to local socialist organizations for financial support, but insisted that there be no strings attached. The answers varied, from 'what has this got to do with winning the next election?' to 'it is not Lenin that you are teaching them'!

The teacher decided that the only future for the educational group method would be if the kids themselves were to carry it on. Once the group had become too cosy, and had mastered what he had to teach, to the point where the kids could argue freely and against him on political matters, then it was time to break it up. And for those who had 'graduated', got a decent job and were no longer kids, it was time to take on the responsibility of new recruits and start a group of their own. After a year John finally took the plunge. He became a revolutionary teacher in his turn. One of his comrades meanwhile set up a group on a nearby estate. The teacher of course works on.

What of the teacher's role in the group? Working outside the school with volunteers as opposed to captives, the teacher had only his own personal authority, and the enthusiasm which group practice generated. Does this mean that his success was dependent on charisma? Or the manipulation of youthful loyalties? Certainly personal qualities of commitment and dedication were called for, which cannot be legislated into existence. But the real question is what form did this commitment, this dedication take.

The relations between the teacher and the group imitated neither the intimacies of close friends nor the indifference of

178

strangers, but was based on the mutual recognition of and respect for the different capabilities that teacher and learner brought to the situation. What happened beyond the group – the love tangles, the falling out of friends, family rows – was of concern only in so far as it jeopardized the life of the group. This was deliberate, intended not out of disregard for the emotional needs and problems of adolescence, but out of a concern to preserve the therapeutic function of the group, that is the comradeship of its working relationships.

In particular the teacher had to maintain the same distance from the learners as from their parents: the distance of the collective educational enterprise he was engaged on, from the family discourse as such; and we might add, it reflects the gap between the socialist enterprise and the working-class ideology. The distance is critical; it allows the young people to establish a distance from a family discourse; it constitutes the symbolic space of an autonomy – to-be-possessed – through which they can find their own voice. This is all the more important when they are subject to emotional binds in their family. The teacher's whole strategy was designed to avoid placing them in situations where they had to choose between their allegiances to the parents and their culture and involvement in the educational group. We should not need to stress the difference between this kind of therapeutic distance between teacher and taught, filled with a warm comradely regard, and that which prevails in the overcrowded classrooms of state education – the distance of reciprocal terrorism.

All this insistence on demarcated positions did not mean that the teacher was permanently locked into the teaching role, while the young remained perennially taught. On the contrary, the group was there to provide revolutionary teachers from its ranks, people who themselves started up groups of their own. This is one way in which a tradition of political education and self-organization can be built up amongst those raised in the neighbourhood, or who are thrown together on the shop floor, and extend outwards as active socialism in the broader struggle of the working class.

If this was possible it was precisely because the educational group was *not* a Marxist study circle, in the manner of the Plebs League, where the 'texts' are studied in talmudic fashion. The group's success lay in the context of its operations – the way it was locked into the reality of working-class life and culture around it. Its success had little to do with having a radical curriculum, innovations in teaching method, or the personal charisma of the teacher.

Such isolated initiatives are like using a bucket to empty an ocean. However, one can envisage how the educational group 'detached teaching' method could be co-opted in new programmes of intervention by enlightened local authorities, independent progressive bodies and their allies. There are dangers – in para-professionalizing the idea, for example. It would be contrary to the selfless principles of such work to create a permanent career hierarchy which tends to produce cosmopolitan élites of peripatetic young professionals with no roots in the areas they are working and motivated only by a diffuse concern to 'work with kids'. And there are pitfalls in seeing existing methods for training teachers and youth workers as automatically appropriate for this kind of work – if for no other reason than that the 'job' involved is so very different.

Educational group work is better suited to the 'born teacher' who has never been near a training college in his life, but who feels at home in the cultural colorations of the environment, than to the paid, qualified professional. The teacher in the above example was just such a volunteer. He came from outside the conventional sources of staffing. There are young married sections of the community who have recently graduated out of the youth scene and may be on the point of retiring hurt into private life, but who feel they have something to give in their free time. The same may apply to retired trade-unionists, with all their valuable knowledge and experience. We would suggest also that all those about to embark on a full-time career in the Labour movement should spend a probationary period in this work. In particular it could provide an important means of training an increasing number of youth officers for trade unions and the Labour movement. When such people leave, some would carry the experience they have gained back into the Labour movement and the welfare state and back into the struggle for their socialist transformation.

Even given these considerations, teachers could not simply be parachuted in to their designated environments. Even when sharing common ground and objectives, the character of their work could not be prescribed by means of a national blueprint. Still less could groups be founded by missionary bands sent out from Centre to preach the socialist gospel. It is necessary to abandon once and for all the evangelical model which has dogged the socialist youth movement throughout its history.

What then is the alternative? Whatever the basis, or lack of it, of material support, the first and essential premise for group work is an approach by a teacher to a local rank and file parent organization, explaining what he has to offer and asking for their support.

The second premise is that there then follows a request to set up a group. Such an initiative would have to entail a commitment to the general principles of the work, and at the same time would constitute an essential condition of support for this kind of intervention. In other words, teachers should not go where they are not invited.

The third premise is an extended period of research and contact work to decide whether the minimum conditions exist for the establishment of a group. This would involve establishing contact with local working-class activists to explain the ideas and enlist and build on their support.

This could be complemented by research into the social and economic history of the area, the state of juvenile employment, and gaining a working knowledge of youth configurations. After all, students may come in as groups rather than individuals. The teacher must have advance warning of the logic behind such solidarities (for example patterns of affinity and emnity) and some sense of their prehistory.

The next step consists in developing contacts with young people themselves. This could move from initially superficial work with a wide spectrum of groupings to more concentrated work with a smaller number of potential cadres. The purpose of the group is explained in terms of getting an educated view of society and developing areas of relevant knowledge and expertise. This may lead to getting a better job or passing exams, but that is not the primary purpose.

The teacher would aim to generate the bulk of his recruits from amongst those who occupy mainstream positions within the local youth culture. At the same time he would seek to draw in the potential survivors from the residual end of the spectrum – those who are not heavily implicated in the déclassé milieus of deviance and its occupational cultures. Of course, it is from amongst those youngsters who for one reason or another find themselves displaced from the dominant instances of working-class life that some of the best cadres may come. In the case of John in the above example, involvement in the educational group was an alternative to the blind alley of purely individualistic solutions, and the marginality this entails. John's rebellion turned inwards against the constraints of the parent culture was replaced into wider political forms of contestation. This does not mean, however, that a youthful career of petty criminality or drug addiction are good credentials in themselves. The teacher is not a rehabilitation officer for those who slip through the safety nets of the welfare state. Young people who in conventional terms are 'most in need', who are a helpless problem to themselves as much as to others, may well be outside his immediate province.

The nucleus that is built up should as far as possible be representative, at least in a sociological sense. It should contain elements of mainstream and residual positions, as well as the subcultural and militant responses to them. It would be dangerous if it were to lean too heavily to one position or another, for example if it were based entirely on a motor-bike gang. For one of the functions of the educational group is to develop through its respective spokesmen an embryonic alliance between otherwise antipathetic groupings. The outcome of this recruitment phase should be a decision, based on all the evidence, of the feasibility or otherwise of running a group on a regular basis.

Even if it's thumbs down, such preliminary work would hardly have been wasted. At best it would help stimulate the creation of a source of youth leadership confident to take initiatives, campaigning for youth representation on the tenants association, setting up a young claimants union, pressuring the council over particular youth issues, producing a youth newspaper, one or two revolutionary teachers. At worst a few kids' heads opened to what's going on about them.

The final phase consists in the establishment of suitable premises and meeting times for the group. A periodization has been suggested but a rigid timetable has not. In fact the likely time span for this group work could be anything from six months to two years, depending on local conditions. It is therefore advisable to concentrate the process of recruitment on the rising fifteen-year-olds, who may be going on seventeen by the time the group gets established. Groups should be small, eight to ten maximum, and meet at least once a week. A visit should also be made to each home, to explain formally to parents about the group, its educational policy, and what Jimmy or Jane will be doing there on Wednesday nights. Groups should be formed on the basis of the teacher's knowledge of individuals (their special circumstances, interests, problems) rather than out of an overriding concern for their sociological composition. Nevertheless, since work would initially be group- rather than curriculum-based, the social chemistry is important. Should everybody in a group already be mates? Should they be of mixed ability? How best to integrate the loners, the handicapped, the shy, and the disruptive? Working youth tend to regard education in their precious disposable time as an imposition. The group would begin by discussing and comparing the different educational experiences of its members; what is wrong with schools, the way things are taught there, and what. This would provide a basis for a general discussion on the value of education and the use to which it is put. But it would be made clear that an educational past was the past, and relative success or failure at school is of no concern here. Areas of extra-curricular knowledge – sport, motor-cycle maintenance, hobbies, as well as latent 'academic' interests – would be explored. In the succeeding weeks each member would be asked to give a short talk, to share his existing knowledge with the group.

Concentrated research should also be attempted in areas of shared knowledge and experience. For example, work experiences and a peer group view of the labour market; official leisure provision, and 'how we really spend our time'; home life and parents' attitudes to their neighbours – alias 'contradictions in the parent culture'. Such basic group work could link to wider and more advanced curriculum-based studies, and this consideration will obviously help determine the composition of each group. A possible curriculum structure might consist of the following basic areas of study: 1) literacy and communication skills; 2) Self health, social biology and sex education; 3) history of working-class life and struggle, local, national and international; 4) studies in applied science and technology. But there are no hard and fast programmes, only decisions to be taken on the ground.

Whatever changes in consciousness arise within the group, it is important that its members do not become displaced from their respective social networks, or the group as a whole become marginalized, because it is precisely in maintaining its links within the mass of local youth that its potential role as a source of leadership must lie.

But, as one of the kids might put it, 'All this talk about education, what about rock 'n' roll?' To take an *a priori* line in group work on the relation between the socialist concept of education and contemporary capitalist youth culture would lead to the crassest puritanism. Consider the following piece of legislation from Lotta Continua, a Marxist group active in the workers' education movement in Italy:

> The red base [i.e. community centre] must also be a place for relaxation. *Though we're not in favour of having things like fruit machines or juke boxes*, there's no reason why boys and girls shouldn't come there to meet, to get to know each other and to work out their problems.

Juke boxes and fruit machines are hardly the most dangerous or effective instruments of exploitation. They may be the symbols of cultural oppression, but they are hardly its substance, and to make this an issue is to lose all sense of strategic priority. Not that these manifestations of commercial youth culture should be exploited – kung fu films after class, to sugar the bitter pill of education. If it is so bitter then there's something wrong with the way it is being done.

Of course there is a tension between rock music as an expression of popular consciousness and its encasement in the youth spectacle; of course the lyrics are sometimes as sexist as the music-hall songs of fifty years ago. But the way to resolve this is not through some moralistic stance over the Bay City Rollers, but by creating an educational context where their value, or lack of it, is thrashed out by the young people themselves.

Internal Order and Popular Justice

It would be idealist to imagine that educational groups would be exempt from the kind of 'trouble' that is associated with more conventional settings – fights, outbreaks of vandalism, thefts, drug problems. We have tried to build controls into the structure and dynamics of the educational group which will ensure the most favourable social chemistry possible. But fortunately the human environment refuses to conform to the laws of experimental physics, and it is neither possible nor desirable to predict or anticipate real events. It would be a great mistake though to interpret internal conflict as always indicating a pathology, a Sign that Something is Wrong. Conflicts of interest or opinion between teacher and students, between groups or individuals, not only will occur but are part of a necessary dialectic of change, without which the educational group would be a dead place. The issue is to make sure that these conflicts are not acted out in a devious or self-destructive way, but instrumentalized through a democratic process. In other words, the issues must be politicized rather than personalized.

This means that there has to be some procedure for rigorously distinguishing these types of conflict from those which result from the carry-over of private feuds, personal rivalries, intrapsychic tensions and group antagonism, conflicts which originate elsewhere, in the family, in the neighbourhood, which lie outside the teacher's scope of intervention, but nevertheless can threaten the group's survival.

All conflict is about power and authority, the relation between them or the lack of them. But conflicts can operate on different levels, that is, they can be real, imaginary, or purely symbolic. So for dealing with problematic situations we need a set of differential procedures, which make explicit in terms of their practice the interpretive rules which are being applied, so that every one knows what is in play, what is at stake, and who is doing what to whom and why. These procedures therefore have to be systematic rather than improvised *ad hoc* solutions to particular events.

What is proceeded from is a Rule, which is a formal proposition about the nature of human co-operation. It states simply that the educational group belongs to its members in so far as they belong to each other; and only in so far as they sustain this comradeship do the members belong individually in the educational group. The circularity of this proposition rests on the paradoxical injunction it contains: be comrades. Evidently comradeship is an objective form of friendship. It is a spontaneous quality. It cannot be enforced or legislated about. Yet it is a conditional rather than an unconditional relationship, the cause and effect of practical solidarity. The rule therefore takes the form of a therapeutic double bind; it ascribes as the function of a given position (the fact of membership) what can only be achieved on a person-to-person basis (the fact of comradeship). But, as against the Scout movement, the rule is made conditional on young people's asserting real, active control over their organizations, rather than the other way round.

Any action which interferes with the objective is damaging to the educational group: for example, actions which attempt to assert imaginary, that is egocentric control, or purely symbolic ones, dissociated 'acting out'. The damage incurred may be physical – smashing a film projector – or moral – giving an interview to a local newspaper, branding the teacher as a trouble-maker. There are any number of ways of 'getting your own back'.

We have already distinguished such oedipal politics from struggles over educational policy. But even where crises arise from the under – or inner – life of the group, there is a further important distinction to be made.

Let us take two common categories of incident. The first could be epitomized by a fight between two lads over a girl, or a punch-up between two rival 'mobs'.

In this situation, by definition, both parties are equally involved and the incident is a product of their ongoing social interaction. The question of right or wrong is entirely relative, and dependent on the punctuation of the event – 'who started it'. But, as common sense has it, in such cases it takes two to tangle, and the issue of punctuation is quite irrelevant, in a strategic sense, to the dynamics of ritual insult and physical injury. So here the teacher alone intervenes, in a role as neutral third party. This intervention must be immediate and tactical; the justice dispensed summary, without appeal, and equivalent on both sides. No arguing the rights and wrongs, simply stop the situation escalating until others take sides.

The second category of incident is no less familiar, but far more pernicious. Petty pilfering, leaving a mess, the mysterious disappearance of essential equipment, smashing up. Such incidents, unless handled correctly, can become endemic, wearing down the idealism of the teacher, creating witch hunts, paranoia amongst the youth and generally immobilizing the collective life. Here it really is a case of right and wrong. Should the recourse be to traditional techniques of popular justice – as with scabs during a strike? Here the guilty party is tried directly by his workmates, and if found guilty, sent to Coventry, fined, beaten up, and so on. For reasons that should be obvious, this would not be workable or appropriate amongst young people. It would only foster duplicity, hostility and division.

Does the teacher call in the law to deal with 'enemies within'?

Alienation of his charges, by what would be a hypocritical recourse; the possibility of the police exploiting the situation; these are two of the consequences of this solution.

What then is the answer? Thumbscrews? Aversion therapy? Heart-to-hearts? Carry on regardless? In our view, the issue is less to extract confessions of guilt, or protestations of innocence (which only isolate the individual), than to bring into play the social processes of pride and shame, collective condemnation and individual self-criticism.

A possible procedure: a teacher's initiative to establish the facts. A discussion confined to all those in any way touched by the injury, whether as victims or possible offenders. In that discussion the teacher delegates the job of coming up with answers to the following questions: Who is responsible? What was the context and motivation? What is to be done by way of reparation? The findings are then presented to the rest of the 'school', all parties to the incident included. The report would have to make clear to what extent the incident is considered symptomatic of a generalized grievance or disaffection from education work – a 'superior' attitude by the teacher, for example – or whether it is an individual act, by a definable culprit or person unknown. If an accusation is made, an opportunity would be given for the accused's side of the case to be put – and perhaps a self-criticism to be made – followed by a general discussion and decision on what is to be done. Undoubtedly such a process would be painful, even humiliating, for those in the hot seat, but this may be attenuated by the support of mates.

A humiliating experience, but not degrading. Pride might be injured, but only to be restored. This all sounds rather painful though, and undoubtedly it would have a deterrent effect. But it does provide a framework of popular justice sufficiently mediated to guard against scapegoating. After all, it is not only in the context of petty crime that individualistic solutions, whether calculating or irrational, would have to be deflected by comradeship, common decencies and socialist ideals.

Young Tenants Associations

So far we have tried to show how education group work could create the conditions for a new source of leadership among working-class youth. One example of such an initiative would be in the emergence of a network of young tenants associations.

The purpose of a young tenants association (YTA) would be both to strengthen existing working-class organizations and to serve the political, cultural and educational needs of the mass of working-class youth in its vicinities. Obviously they could flourish only where the demographic structure of an area allowed, for example where there were a large number of middle-aged parents and a large number of their teenage children. A 'new' town such as Milton Keynes, with its overwhelming preponderance of young marrieds, however, would have to wait ten years before a YTA was even a possibility.

Given these preconditions, how would YTAs come into being and on what basis? Let us take four possible contexts for their emergence:

YTAs might be formed in opposition to TAs and other parental bodies which had a record of being hostile to youth interests and needs. Or they might be set up as a result of a youth initiative on an estate in parallel to a moribund parent organization. A similar initiative could see the emergence of a tenants association dominated by the young on an estate where, as in the vast majority of cases, no such organization existed before, or where one has become defunct. Finally, there is that tiny minority of TAs usually formed in struggle, for example rent strikes, and often confined to occupational communities (Clay Cross, Merseyside) which are strong and militant. Here the demand for YTAs could be translated as more active youth sections, ably supported by the parents.

In all these contexts, hopefully, educational group work could have a decisive impact. In the story of the Black Horse, for example, where conditions emerged – virtually spontaneously –

for a YTA to be formed after a confrontation with the openly hostile Open Space Committee, educational group work could have provided a renewed source of youth leadership and adult counselling, as well as support for those leaders like Brian who were actually thrown up in the struggle. This would be in contrast to his probably permanent political disillusionment as the Committee successfully exploited the latent divisions amongst the kids, many of whom turned against him. Here the tactic we suggest, of bringing together those representing a broad spectrum of positions amongst local youth into educational group work, could, over time, play its part in solidifying the YTA.

Even if these things had happened on the Monmouth, there would have been nowhere for the YTA to meet unsupervised by adults, except for the hotly contested space of the Black Horse. So here, a youth house in the vicinity could have been campaigned for and would have provided a more permanent and conducive base for activity.

As well as providing a platform for specific youth issues, one of the main aims of the YTAs, whatever their context, would be to promote active youth representation and involvement in the tenants' movement as a whole, not to oppose it. Where a YTA paralleled a hostile or unresponsive parent body, the latter's committees could at least be awakened to the reality of specific youth needs and demands. As a result, some might retire gracefully making way for a more dynamic leadership, or they might simply co-opt some young tenants on to their committee. In our view, such organized outcomes to adult chauvinist attitudes could only be healthy for the tenants' movement; rather than the chronic feuds and personal vendettas between the generations often drawing on the wounds of family life – a rational working-through of the conflict.

But what of tenants associations which are simply moribund, as incapable of dealing with the kids as they are with the needs of their adult members, *vis-à-vis* the authorities. If YTAs are to play their part in rejuvenating the tenants' movement successfully, then our proposed intervention must ensure that they do not mirror, either in form or in content, this all-too familiar aspect of its disintegration. And certainly not if they wish to capture the imagination.

Would YTAs employ a platform, constitutions, strict procedural rules for meetings, for example, as is the case with their elders? On the Monmouth, the TA Committee used all these things to defuse the spontaneity of a youthful audience. This is not to suggest that constitutionality, points of order and the rest is compatible with our concept of YTAs. Initially they would have their place; but in the long run the success of a broad young tenants' movement would depend on the ability of adult counsellors to suggest, through educational group work, other organizational structures which already have some basis in the members' spontaneity.

Nor would it be always appropriate for YTAs to mirror the single estate model organization of most TAs. On the Monmouth, the TA committee, concerned solely with the affairs of 'our estate', treated their neighbours with as much distance as the GLC (and there was little sense of being part of a wider movement). But the kids did not fit so neatly into these demarcations. A YTA, then, could be supra-local – its informal networks extending into several neighbouring estates, schools and workplaces.

In that most likely of contexts for the emergence of YTAs, a youth initiative (adult-encouraged), when no TA exists at all, the raising of supra-local issues, such as schools' campaigns channelled through educational groups, could be a decisive factor for their socialist development. For otherwise there is the tendency in these cases simply to take over the functions and concerns of what would have been an adult TA, and this may even include acting as vigilantes against the teenage rampage.

On the other side of the borough from the Monmouth estate, the Orme Court TA was the 'youngest in Britain', the average age of its members eighteen. It started after a youth worker, having set up a club in the middle of the estate, managed to direct the energies of his members on to community issues. Walls were cleaned up, a help-the-aged scheme started, and a militant campaign launched against the council to have a dangerous road closed. The youth worker was able to find a core leadership for all this among young, about-to-be-marrieds looking for respectability and status in this rough neighbourhood and tearaways wishing to reform (the youth worker was himself an ex-borstal boy). What this core group represented was a rejection of both subcultural and individual solutions and a shift away from residual, towards mainstream, positions. As a TA they were militantly anti-council. As a youth committee, they reacted strongly to the anarchy and violence of the youth scene. 'We were sick of all the violence and smashing up . . . we decided to do something about it ourselves . . . taking pride in our estate.'

While a definite blow for youth's right to a voice in neighbourhood affairs, the Orme Court TA showed little concern for wider political issues, stressing always its concentration on civic matters (pride in the appearance of the estate). This meant that there was often as little purchase on any wider social reality outside the estate as on the Monmouth.

Educational group work, the influence of their adult counsellors, would try to ensure that a young tenants' movement would retain much of the Orme Court TA's militancy over civic matters while placing them in a broader political context. Rather than a series of localist backlash organizations, it would be a movement with a strong pull in the geopolitics of youth and a strong push against the authorities.

Here are some scenarios of what such a movement as is envisaged here could do, some possible ways it might react to everyday youth issues and needs.

Frustration, discrimination, exploitation, bullying . . .
There's nothing to do round here in the evenings. The YTA gets its disco and the licensee is forced to lift his ban on teenagers. A café where amphetamines are being pushed to little kids is 'blacked', and so is a commercial disco which overcharges, or a sports centre which puts up its admission charges without consultation. A particular copper has a reputation for picking on kids . . . The YTA brings things like this to public notice. Calls for his removal from the area, or from the force.

Trouble with school, work, getting dole, finding a place to live . . .
There's too much use of the cane, we're forced to wear uniforms.
The best teacher in the school has been sacked. YTA members
still at neighbourhood school and sympathetic teachers form
their action group and organize with YTA sponsorship. No rise
for two years in print shop, apprentice hair stylist turns out to be
a polite term for someone to clean up the salon. The YTA presses
for action from relevant trade unions. A claimants union organizer comes down to inform those out of work of their rights . . .
a young claimants union emerges. Then there are the national
issues, public housing, provision for single youth, lowering the age
of consent, free abortion on demand.

Educating the parents . . .
Some disapproving tenants keep chivvying the kids. Long hair
and drugs, it's disgusting. Your mother should be locked up for
letting a girl your age wear dresses like that. Playing football in the
streets? We'll set the police on you. Incipient vigilante actions.
Keep off the grass and stay off. We don't want the likes of you
round here. A petition circulates to pressure the council to produce mobile anti-vandal patrols.

The YTA retaliates by investigating complaints, organizing a
forum where these issues can be thrashed out, and even calling for
more provision for housebound old people. The aim is not to
intensify age chauvinism on either side, but to create a public
realm of discussion where for once the slap in the face for coming
home late countered by Led Zeppelin blasting out at two in the
morning will not work.

Backing each other up . . .
A girl gets thrown out of home because her boyfriend is supposed
to be a bad influence. Someone has been mistakenly singled out in
a take-and-drive away case. A member is pressurized by parents
or police to leave the YTA. Although never interfering where it
is not invited, the YTA would be encouraged by adult counsellors
to make expressions of practical solidarity in cases such as these.
'Never meet them alone.' The next time a member gets picked on,
YTA members try to bail him out. If anyone is sent to prison,

thrown out of home, or in hospital, the YTA would make sure that at least they get visited and contacts are kept up.

Team rivalry . . .
A series of confrontations and stand offs between rival 'mobs' is threatened. Police and social workers are alerted. Press and right-wing politicians circle around. The YTA intervenes, neither as a rival mob, nor as a rival agency of social control. Behind the scenes, through their informal networks, they attempt to mediate. Hopefully, over time, the growth of a young tenants' movement would act to defuse all these all-too-familiar scenarios.

The Youth Newspaper: A Case in Point

One place where the educational, cultural and political aspects of this whole programme link concretely is in the production of a youth newspaper. This would not be a house magazine, produced by and for resident educational group cadres and affiliates, but would have a wider appeal. The place where Jimmy Reid can meet the Stretford End, and Powellism and Roller mania get their come-uppance . . . One can envisage how its production would deploy a wide range of skills in verbal and visual literacy.

In the Black Horse, for example, a youth newspaper, proudly entitled *The Duke*, was produced, and we had no difficulty in finding designers, photographers, record buffs, interviewers and jokesmiths. But in this case its appeal was largely that of an interesting diversion, for some simply an opportune means of getting one's name before the public – rather than a serious attempt to militate to a wider audience. Besides, as abortive attempts at distribution proved, despite the horror comic hero on the cover and controversial features on violence at the Riverside Sports Centre, the sheer amateurishness of its presentation compared with more professionally produced rivals ensured that its readers would be confined to those who produced it and their close friends.

At the founding meeting of the newspaper we passed around a representative sample of publications, both commercial and evangelical, aimed specifically at youth. From militant broad-sheets such as *Challenge* and *Keep Left*, to their free press equivalents such as *Y-Front* and *Aggro*, to Westerns, *Mirabelle* and *Shoot*. Would our headlines exhort the entire working class to bring capitalism to its knees and youth to play its part in redoubling its efforts to sell the paper? Or would we sound an angry populist note, fired by reports of local kids getting together fighting back against the system? Or would we be more consciously do-it-yourself, reflecting an irreverent 'up yours' attitude to politics? Or would we shun politics altogether, and stick to pin-ups of dreamy-eyed heroes, Goal-of-the-Month competitions and the agonies of teenage romance?

In the event the form and content of the Black Horse newspaper was determined by those who got most actively involved in its production, and something of all these tendencies was reflected. On one page, jokes and a comic strip, on the next *Down with Skool*, *Arsenal Rules*, and a picture of someone's girlfriend. And of course there were many different styles of writing involved. It is here that the impact of educational group work in our programme should play its part, in sharpening the style and stance of youthful journalism, while experience gained in an educational group or in a young tenants association would widen such a paper's social concerns. From a house mag miscellany produced for the delectation of its contributors, to a place where their consciousness meets those of their peers outside without either being self-consciously juvenile, or having a prematurely middle-aged concern for national politics to the exclusion of youth matters.

No matter how exciting the content, the effectiveness of the youth newspaper as a class weapon depends on its relation with its readership. Who would read it? How would it be distributed? How could youth get access to contribute? These are questions that cannot be answered by pointing to sales figures alone (indeed, they are often obscured by them).

Ever since the rise of the mass newspaper, however, the Left has tended to think otherwise. 'Build the mass party through the mass circulation daily.' To a concept of the Party which opposed the class-conscious vanguard to the less advanced rank and file corresponds the concept of the newspaper with its professional band of committed journalists, with their predetermined editorial party line, opposed to an atomized, anonymous readership. In Britain, traces of this model still survive, as Left groups try to emulate in theory at least the 'fighting dailies' of the 1920s. But Left youth publications especially, despite the challenge of their names, share a tiny circulation, and tend to reflect a purely sectarian reality. In effect, house magazines for those in the know. One of the key *rites de passage* for young people into the world of socialist politics is still 'selling the paper'. Standing on the corner, watching the girls go by, on a cold winter evening (or at least it always feels like that). A brave stance amidst the waves of grim-faced commuters. 'Advance!' 'Forward!' 'Keep Left!' 'Help kick out the Tories!' Get your copies now, as the crowd swerve to one side or the other.

The trouble with trying to build a youth movement around a newspaper is that circulation becomes the main yardstick of success – invariably more and more effort is put in for less and less return. A more effective model would have to settle on a method of distribution which would spare its youngsters the disillusioning experience of street-selling socialism.

So the youth newspaper starts small, its distribution built on informal social networks radiating out from the educational group. As the range of content expands, so too the audience it commands; as active involvement grows, so too the network of distribution.

A small-scale operation. Yet anything larger depends on it. Thriving local mags would be a vital prerequisite for a socialist youth newspaper anywhere near able to contest the domination of the market by the stable of commercial teen mags whose circulation totals over a million and whose readership must be several times that.

Postscript: Figures in a Political Landscape

1972. GLENN FORD, eighteen. Born and brought up in North London; mother left home when he was still a child (she was an addict of Western films, and for this reason the child was called Glenn). Father, a dustman, married again, to an industrious, houseproud woman. They lived in a small two-up, two-down, in a street inhabited almost entirely by immigrants. Most family talk about the world outside centred on crude race hatred and stereotyping. In 1970, Mr and Mrs Ford voted for the National Front in the general election. Glenn suffered from dyslexia, but this went undiagnosed. He was classified as educationally subnormal in his primary school and was later placed in the remedial stream of the comprehensive. He left school at fifteen with no qualifications; got a job in a small firm of furniture makers near to his home. Soon objected to the long hours, the pitiful wages the broken promises of a rise. Started to ask questions of his workmates, took his demands to the boss. No response. Finally, 'went on a one-man work-to-rule . . . if you won't allow me to join a union, I'll form one of my own.' Was sacked on the spot.

A chastening experience. When he got another job, as a labourer on a building site, he joined UCATT. Started to teach himself to read. Every evening after work, he went to the children's section of the public library. Beginning with Donald Duck, he mastered the books for five-to-sevens, graduated to older children's literature, and on from there. A slow, painful process. In 1971 he went along to an advertised meeting of the local branch of the Young Communist League. He found the people there more interesting than his old mates. He was well liked, and renowned for his boozing prowess. Before he joined the YCL there had been no one to whom he had been particularly close.

He formed a strong friendship with another member, who was a student at the local college of further education.

Stopped speaking to his dad. YCL activities rapidly became the centre of his life. He was an enthusiastic newspaper-seller and leafleteer. Enjoyed street arguments, and was good at repartee. He particularly enjoyed 'having a go at white racists', who approached him while he was selling papers outside the tube. 'I learned to fight racism from fighting my dad.' Turned out for all demos, was elected secretary of the local Angela Davis Defence Group. Would read every Left-wing political pamphlet he could lay his hands on, but also read novels – Dickens, Kafka, Orwell . . . Although he had difficulty reading Marx, he managed to acquire a basic understanding of Marxist theory – 'The bosses will only employ you if they can make a profit out of you . . .' – and this seemed to attune to his sharply materialistic sense of the world. But the basis of his political outlook was 'anti-Tory, anti-Fascist'. He was sceptical about the Communist Party, although reluctant to criticize it publicly. He saw the ponderous bureaucracy, and all the other failings of the Communist Party, as 'a bit of a laugh'. He referred to the CP affectionately as 'the old Party', to himself as 'one of the red thugs'. He did not take the Party's pro and anti Soviet controversy too seriously. As far as he was concerned, 'it's not paradise, I know, but they don't have unemployment there.' Although he would argue publicly that the task of the Party was to 'strengthen class solidarity' etc., privately his cynicism about working-class political attitudes seemed to have been strengthened after joining the YCL. 'It's a way out, the Party, in this branch most of the members are workers . . . but you can talk freely, express yourself, learn things from each other. Arguing with a six-foot navvy on the lump, you come away wondering either I'm mad or he's mad.'

His socialism, then, separated him from the 'irrational, ignorant, violent' sides of working-class life, and his working-class 'mateyness' became a mask for his rationality and intellectual purpose, all the heavy drinking and swearing something of a calculated performance.

In 1972 the branch secretary of his union died. Glenn was elected in his place (the support of a single comrade being enough to swing the vote). Branch secretary at eighteen! But the demands of the post threatened to impose severe demands on his powers of literacy. He would have to take notes, read minutes, formulate proposals, write leaflets, attend AGMs, and although he had taught himself to read, he still could not write fluently. The union sent him to evening classes. The first target was English O-level. After that, who knows? A scholarship to Ruskin College? He would have little trouble reaching the necessary intellectual standard, but the physical act of forming individual letters, then whole sentences, still troubled him.

His pet hates were the 'bunch of Trotskyist students who have taken over the local trades council'. 'They are troublemakers, but the workers hate them.' Sneered at 'long-haired hippies and middle-class trendies', and was untouched by youth fashions and youth culture generally, without being old-fashioned. Grew a beard, wore big boots and a donkey jacket, maintained an affable front to the world. A young worker, representative of a dwindling minority, for whom socialist politics was the centre of life.

Five years separate the political awakening of Glenn Ford from that of BARRY WATTS, eighteen-year-old voter for the National Front in the 1977 GLC elections. Like Glenn, Barry was born and brought up in North London. His father, a bricklayer, settled there from Ireland after the war. In 1970, after several years on the housing list, the family were moved out of their terraced back street on to a big council estate which had a high concentration of West Indians and Asians. Pride and relief at having finally got a decent place to live soon turned sour because of this. 'You see them natives on TV, dancing around in the jungle. I [Barry] says, we got 'em living next door to us. We don't like that. Their music, the food, the smell, they're different, their whole attitude to life is different to ours. You got to put a gas mask on to get past their door.'

Such blind prejudice may have been due to the latent insecurity of this London Irish family, but it was also spurred by the fact that unemployed blacks were responsible for much of the crime in

199

the area – because of them it was 'unsafe to walk around alone at night'. When an elderly relative had her bag snatched by a black kid, Mr Watts asked, was this the better life that he had worked so hard for? Haven't people the right to choose who they want to live with, and who they don't? The power to answer these questions seemed to lie with 'the politicians' . . .

The Watts were lifelong Labour voters. Mr Watts had considered himself a socialist in his youth, while his wife had once been elected shop steward in her factory. 'But Labour aren't doing or saying anything about it. They just defend them [the blacks].' Yet neither could bring themselves to vote Conservative. It was left to their son to break this political impasse.

At school Barry had been placed in the lower streams, where most of his classmates were coloured, and some could barely speak English. A slightly built lad, he was known for his 'gift of the gab', and for getting into fights; not just with the black kids. He was picked out as a Manchester United supporter in this Arsenal stronghold, and for being Irish (this was the time of the IRA London bombing campaign). He always prided himself that he never backed out of fights, and one time he was badly beaten up after taking on too many opponents at once. In the end the only things he had to show for five years' 'education' were a broken nose and a lot of bumps and bruises.

Barry's first contact with the National Front had been at the age of fourteen, during a pupils' strike at his school. A man hanging around outside the school gates had handed him a leaflet blaming 'the coloureds' for the lack of discipline and the drop in educational standards. Unlike most of his mates, Barry was impressed. A crude explanation was being offered here both for his school's oppressive, violent atmosphere and for his own conspicuous lack of success. At the same time his gut anger and hatred against black people had hardened. 'I broke my arm. I had to go to the hospital. There was a Paki doctor. I wouldn't let him near me. I asked for someone else. They make me feel sick . . .'

Out of work for nearly a year after leaving school, Barry started to attend Front meetings and read their literature. He mastered all their narrow scapegoating arguments – 'it's the wogs that are taking our jobs', etc. In his first job, in a warehouse, and on the terraces with his fellow United supporters, he became a fluent and passionate advocate for the NF. In the spring of 1977, to the surprise of his father, and the express disapproval of his mother, he went on a much-publicized Front demonstration in North London.

There was this big green near Haringey Stadium. There was thousands of 'em [anti-Front marchers], waiting. This geezer came over, gave me a leaflet. It said Asians, all that lot, together with Whites. I gave it 'im back. I didn't wanna know. They were throwing bottles at us. Then this van comes along, saying get the National Front off the streets and all this. Then some kid behind me put a brick through the window screen. Then coloured and whites come over. Half of us started to walk away, started to go on the march. If it wasn't for the coppers there – the coppers save your life. There were lots of whites, though, with the blacks, against us. I don't care if I get done over. I'm proud of it. Half the trouble is the whites are scared to come out and support us.

A few weeks later came the Greater London Council elections.

My dad didn't know I was gonna vote. On my way home from work I saw the polling station. Then I got my dad to come with me. We both voted Front. He usually votes Labour. It was always my opinion, not my dad's, to support the Front. I got him to change his mind. My mother she still don't approve. She thinks they're a load of rubbish. She says they'll never get elected. But she goes, 'It's up to you what you vote. You go your own way.' She still votes Labour. I argue with her. We all do.

Barry recognizes his mother's fears about the Front. He dislikes being called a fascist and is not totally wide-eyed about the leadership:

I know the Front may cause evil things in the future – when they get power – but if you go on that march, we was peaceful, we didn't do nothing.

Still, he is proud of the Front's reputation as 'the hatred party' – 'because *they* hate us. They won't be just mugging us, they'd be shooting us if they had their way.'

Postscript: Figures in a Political Landscape

Evenings, Barry and a group of mates patrol the streets, daubing walls with NF slogans, or set upon coloured workers coming home alone from nearby factories. 'But it's black and white, blokes and women, seeing them together, I hate that. That's the worst.' One night, Barry was arrested for 'causing an affray' after spitting at a couple in the street . . .

Many socialists would argue that lads like Glenn are the 'salt of the earth' while Barry's is a sick, fascistic mentality which has to be either 'treated' or crushed. Yet there are positive points of comparison. Both decided to fight back against the institutionalized violence of a social and economic system that threatened to crush them. Barry even shares some of Glenn's anti-capitalist ideals.

We're for the old folks, we're for them. We think they should get a better deal. And the kiddies, somewhere for them to play. Better schools . . . The Labour government, they are out to help the rich, they are all for the people with the money.

The real difference is that Glenn, at the beginning of the seventies, under a Tory government and with a miners' strike threatened, studied hard to equip himself to look beyond narrow local class and family confines – and the YCL milieu helped him to do this. Barry, on the other hand, remains locked into the all-too-real racist divisions within his own neighbourhood, and this forms the basis for his political mobilization – he acts out with a vengeance all the repressed chauvinist feelings of the parent culture against 'the black invaders'. (His own position as a part-outsider struggling to be more British than the British obviously helps here.)

Is all this just a matter of individual consciousness? Or are there political and educative interventions which could provide the support the kids lack, which could broaden their horizons without displacing them from their community, and which would help neutralize the appeal of Right-wing populism and minimize the activities of lads like Barry? The question is urgent. In 1972 Glenn Ford learned to fight racism by fighting his dad; he joined